DESTINY

Who you are
and what you're
here to do

Also by Karl Haffner:
Cure for Soul Fatigue
Diaper University
Pilgrim's Problems
Soul Matters

The author would love your feedback!
Share your thoughts, stories, and pictures with Karl:

karlhaffner@gmail.com
www.karlhaffner.com
Twitter: @karlhaffner
Facebook: Karl Haffner
Instagram: karlhaffner

To order, call **1-800-765-6955.**
Visit us at **www.reviewandherald.com** for information on other
Review and Herald® products.

DESTINY

Who you are
and what you're
here to do

Karl Haffner

REVIEW AND HERALD® PUBLISHING ASSOCIATION
Since 1861 | www.reviewandherald.com

Published by Review and Herald® Publishing Association, Hagerstown, MD 21741-1119

This book was
Edited by Gerald Wheeler
Copyedited by Amy Prindle
Cover designed by Daniel Anez / Review and Herald® Design Center
Cover art by © Thinkstock.com
Interior designed by Emily Ford / Review and Herald® Design Center
Typeset: Minion Pro 11/13

PRINTED IN U.S.A.

17 16 15 14 13   5 4 3 2 1

Library of Congress Cataloging-in-Publication Data
Haffner, Karl, 1961- .
  Destiny : who you are and what you're here to do / Karl Haffner.
    p. cm.
1. Christian life—Seventh-Day Adventist authors. I. Title.
  BV4501.3.H3425 2013
  248.4'86732—dc23
                    2012032262

ISBN 978-0-8280-2700-7

Every once in a while God plops people in our lives
who redefine the meaning of supportive.
Fred and Mary Kaye Manchur
have been those people for me.

Thank you for the invitation to be a part of the Kettering journey.
I admire your inspiring commitment to the church.
I appreciate your leadership in our community.
And I am deeply grateful for your friendship.

Some **people I appreciate . . .**

The Wareham tribe—for cheerfully helping with everything—from moving pianos to proofing my manuscript. Marshall, Karen, Elizabeth, and Grant, you are superhuman! If I could arrange for the Cubs to win the World Series for you, Grant, you know I would. But alas! I'm no performer of miracles.

The incredible team of pastors at Kettering church—you make the office a great place to hang out.

Kay—the consummate expression of grace and glue for my scattered life.

Andy and Danny—without you my computer would be terminally on strike.

Dwain—the curriculum guru who is the reason for this book.

Raj—the greatest conference president in the galaxy (including Ohio).

Brett—who sees me at my quadruple bogie worst and still treats me like a par.

Cherié, Lindsey, and Claire—my favorite women on the planet.

Contents

Introduction
Destiny or Dust?   11

Who Am I?
Are You Smarter Than a Smartphone?   17
Holy Memoir! I Am God's Kid   20
Saint Me: I Am a Saint   24
Dual Citizenship: I Am a Colonist   32

Why Am I Here?
Existential Answers From Einstein, Tutu, Pinocchio . . .   41
A Mist Not to Be Missed   45
Two Cents of Significance   52
I Will Never Happen Again   59
Dying Rich Versus Living Rich   65
On Purpose   74
"How Can I Know God's Will?" and Other Confusing Questions   80
Church Matters   88

Where Am I Going?
YOU: On a Tombstone   97
Blessed Assurance   106
Safe at Home   111
A Trip That's Out of This World   116

Conclusion
Po or Purpose?   123

Introduction
Destiny or Dust?

In giving the commencement address at Harvard University, comedian Will Ferrell concluded by singing a song. "'Dust in the wind,'" he moaned like a moose in heat. "'All we are is dust in the wind. Dust in the wind, all we are is dust in the wind.'"

Midsong he caught himself and said, "OK, you know what? I'm just realizing that this is a terrible graduation song. . . . This is the first time I've actually listened to the lyrics. Man, it's a downer. It's bleak."

Ferrell then crinkled his face as if he were concocting new lyrics on the fly. He sang again: "Now don't hang on, nothing lasts forever but the Harvard alumni endowment fund. It adds up, has performed at 22 percent growth over the last six years. Dust in the wind, you're so much more than dust in the wind. Dust in the wind, you're shiny little very smart pieces of dust in the wind."

For Real?

Do you reckon he was right? The Bible does say, "For dust you are and to dust you will return" (Gen. 3:19).

Is that it? Dust in the wind? Is that the sum of your significance?

The main character in the movie *Antz* also wonders about this. The opening scene has the ant named Z postured on a leaf couch, talking to a therapist:

"All my life I've lived and worked in the big city," he says. "I always tell myself there has got to be something better out there. Maybe I . . . maybe I think too much. I think everything must go back to the fact that I had a very anxious childhood. My mother never had time for me. When you're the middle child in a family of 5 million, you don't get any attention. I mean, how is it possible? I've always had these abandonment issues, which plagued me.

My father was basically a drone, like I've said. The guy flew away when I was just a larva. And my job—don't get me started on it, because it really annoys me. I was not cut out to be a worker. I . . . I feel physically inadequate. My whole life I've never been able to lift more than 10 times my own body weight. And when you get down to it, handling dirt is not my idea of a rewarding career. . . . The whole system makes me feel . . . insignificant."

"Excellent!" the therapist squeals. "You've made a real breakthrough!"

"I have?" Z is surprised.

"Yes, Z. You *are* insignificant!"

The next scene shows millions of worker ants all doing the same task—each one carrying dirt. As Z goes to his workstation he says to himself, "OK, I've just got to keep a positive attitude; a good attitude—even though I'm utterly insignificant. I'm insignificant, but with attitude."

Here . . . for What?

Is that it? So long as we've got attitude, maybe we shouldn't fret about our insignificant, dusty little lives. But who wants to waste their life just moving dirt around? It is unconscionable—even inhumane.

Consider the form of torture that has proved to be menacingly effective during wartime. It happens when his captors tell a prisoner of war to dig a deep hole—one that may take days to do. Upon completion, when the prisoner is just beginning to feel the satisfaction of a job well done, he receives a command to fill it in and start excavating another one just like it, only a few feet away. When he finishes that hole, he is forced to shovel the dirt back in and start a third one.

At first glance you might suppose such punishment to be more humane than most. After all, the prisoner does not get whipped, starved, or intimidated at gunpoint. It involves good exercise. Sometimes there is sunshine. Nonetheless, psychologists say that it's only a matter of time before the prisoner goes clinically insane. Why?

Obviously it is because the work serves no purpose. Tell that same prisoner to dig a 50-mile drainage ditch, all by himself, to move sewage away from an orphanage. He could labor on such a purposeful task for years without going mad. But simply to move dirt with no meaningful end in mind is persecution at its peak.

In the end, nobody aspires to a life of meaningless dirt management. Who wants to be a speck of dust that flits though the world without a hint of significance? You and I were created for more.

"For we are God's handiwork," the Bible teaches, "created in Christ Jesus to do good works, which God prepared in advance for us to do" (Eph. 2:10).

God created you. You are not dust in the wind, nor are you an insignificant ant in need of psychotherapy. Instead, you were "created in Christ Jesus to do good works." Notice that the text does not say that God made you to haul dirt around without purpose. God prepared you in advance to do good—to make a difference. And it is upon this foundational truth that we will explore the big questions everyone must answer:

Who am I?

Why am I here?

Where am I going?

Together we will explore the tricky terrain of emergent faith, religion, calling, purpose, meaning—the big-picture concerns that underlie the earthy stuff that consumes our calendars: school, work, marriage, kids; the list goes on and on. Without focus on your destiny, however, those chores start to feel like digging holes only to be filled in again—busyness with no purpose.

Please join me in this journey as we explore the pathway of purpose that God has uniquely paved for you. It may get muddy, and there will be ruts, rocks, and hurdles along the way. But to press on toward God's ideal is to partner with the Creator of the universe to fulfill the intrinsic function for which He created *you*, and only you. The objective here is to live the life you were meant to live.

So let's get living!

Who **Am I?**

*"Any life, no matter how long and complex it may be,
is made up of a single moment—the moment in which a man finds out,
once and for all, who he is."*

—Jorge Luis Borges

"It's never too late to be what you might have been."

—George Eliot

*"People can't live with change if there's not a changeless core inside them.
The key to the ability to change is a changeless sense of who you are, what
you are about and what you value."*

—Stephen R. Covey

*"Be who you are and say what you feel, because those who mind don't
matter, and those who matter don't mind."*

—Dr. Seuss

*"Always remember that you are absolutely unique.
Just like everyone else."*

—Margaret Mead

*"If you don't know who you are, a university
is an expensive place to find out."*

—A. Armstrong

Are You Smarter Than a Smartphone?

W ho am I?"
Input that question to Siri, the computer-generated know-it-all that lives in the iPhone 4s, and she'll answer, "I don't know who you are; but you can tell me."

Shucks. I was hoping she would have the answer and I could start my next book. But alas, I guess my smartphone ain't that smart. Not only does Siri fail to answer my question, she puts the onus on me to tell her who I am. If only it was that easy.

"Who am I? That is a simple question, yet it is one without a simple answer," writes Demetri Martin in *The New Yorker.* "I am many things—and I am one thing. But I am not a thing that is just lying around somewhere, like a pen, or a toaster, or a housewife. That is for sure. I am much more than that. I am a living, breathing thing, a thing that can draw with a pen and toast with a toaster and chat with a housewife, who is sitting on a couch eating toast. And still, I am much more."[1]

A group of psychologists once asked people to write down 20 answers to the question "Who am I?" Interestingly, children tended to say things like "I am a girl/boy"; "I am 10 years old"; "I am blond"; etc. Adults were more inclined to include such things as "I am a teacher/secretary/manager"; "I am a mother/father/daughter/son"; "I am a good friend"; etc. In other words, kids were more likely to offer descriptive terms, while adults' answers were more likely to respond in terms of social roles and relationships.[2]

Regardless of how you answer the question, it is a vital one. If you are to fulfill your God-ordained destiny, it is critical to have clarity on your identity.

Looking for Yourself in All the Wrong Places

When it comes to finding out who you are, you will find many people eager to aid you. Self-help experts, talk show hosts, maharishis, and counselors—all are keen to assist you as you explore your inner being. But they send you searching in the wrong place. "Look within," they say.

"But the promise of self-discovery falls short," claims Max Lucado. "Can you find the plot of a book in one paragraph or hear the flow of a symphony in one measure? Can you uncover the plot of your life by examining your life? By no means. You are so much more than a few days between the womb and the tomb."[3]

There's more to your life than your life. The answer to the question "Who am I?" makes sense only when placed in a broader context. Who you are is relative to who God is. In His broader, sweeping saga you play a crucial role.

"It's in Christ that we find out who we are and what we are living for. Long before we first heard of Christ and got our hopes up, he had his eye on us, had designs on us for glorious living, part of the overall purpose he is working out in everything and everyone" (Eph. 1:11, 12, Message).

Let's be clear: you are a part of God's overall purpose. Finding it, though, isn't an event—it is an ongoing, constant journey that unfolds each day as you live in Christ. Remember Paul's statement: "It's in Christ that we find out who we are."

Looking for Yourself in the Right Person

In Christ we discover our identity, our destiny and our place in His story. It is in Him that we belong. Without this God perspective, our lives become pointless. Futile. Desperate. We feel alone, like Rachael:

I met her at a Week of Prayer. After the final meeting she tentatively approached me and asked, "Pastor Haffner, may I speak to you?"

The first thing that struck me about this 10-year-old was her sweater. It was a really hot day—not the kind you'd expect to see such clothing.

"Sure," I smiled, "I'd be glad to talk to you. What's on your mind?"

I was not emotionally prepared for her story.

"Well," she dropped her gaze and began, "I'm very sad because my best friend threw herself in front of a truck because she didn't want to live anymore. Her classmates nicknamed her Hippo Hillary. She didn't like being fat, so she jumped off a bridge into a truck. It happened last year, and I've been very sad ever since. I really miss her."

You can understand how my heart hurt for Rachael. I asked if she had good support in her family. "I don't know," she shrugged. "My dad is never home, and my mom just tells me to grow up and get over it. My brother drinks a lot. We're not very close."

"How about friends at school?" I probed.

"Well, Hillary was my best friend. When she died, it was as if I didn't have any close friend to replace her."

"What about at church?"

"I don't go to church."

"You feel alone?"

Nodding, she stared at her sneakers.

For the next two hours we talked. I assured her that deep feelings of despair were not unusual given her life experiences. I promised to follow up with some resources she might find helpful. Mostly, however, I just cried for her and told her how much God loves her.

"Rachael, all your friends and family may ditch you," I said, "but Jesus will never leave you. He's crazy about *you*, and He has big plans for you."

Toward the end of our conversation she made an unusual comment. She intimated that her hobby was hurting herself. A few questions later she pulled up the sleeve of her sweater.

I gasped. Her arm was a spiderweb of cuts.

"Whenever I cry, I cut myself until I can't feel the tears anymore."

Rachael is not someone I will soon forget. Her story reminds me of how vital it is for us to know that we are loved and that we do belong. We belong to Christ, and we belong in this world. Every one of us has a part in His redemptive story. In Christ we find the authoritative answer to the question "Who am I?"

---

[1] Demetri Martin, "Who am I?" *The New Yorker*, Feb. 28, 2011, www.newyorker.com/humor/2011/02/28/110228sh_shouts_martin?currentPage=all (accessed Feb. 29, 2012).

[2] Florence Mackenzie, *Destructive Emotions: Facing Up to Guilt, Fear, and Anger* (Pleasant Word, 2007), p. 15, www.equippedforliving.org/pdfs/destructive/Chapter%202.pdf (accessed Feb. 29, 2012).

[3] Max Lucado, *God's Story, Your Story* (Grand Rapids: Zondervan, 2011), pp. 24, 25.

Holy Memoir!
I Am God's Kid

Who are you? You have six words to answer the question.

A phenomenon all the rage recently is *Six-Word Memoirs*. It's a game, it's a book, it's a Web site. Even *Oprah* magazine has featured it—does it get any bigger than that? This very simple concept involves telling your life story in six words. Consider a few of the millions of stories:

"Never really finished anything except cake."—Carletta.

"15,000 days spent considering a belly button."—Anstey.

"Many risky mistakes, very few regrets"—Richard.

"Made a mess, found God's grace!"—MsVeeJay1.

"Yes, my life has a purpose!"—Deliadelia.

On the Leonard Lopate radio program aired on February 27, 2009, a girl named Anne shared her six-word memoir: "I found my mother's suicide note." She shared how important it was for her to deal with her mother's death, and the role of that note in the process. Her mom left six words: "No flowers, no funeral, no nothing."[1]

Pretty dark summary of a life, don't you think?

The six-word memoirs got me thinking. In a half dozen words, who am I? Who are you?

Who You Are

The apostle John needed but six words to answer that question for all of us: "We are called children of God" (1 John 3:1, NCV).

That's it! My story. Your story. We are the children of God.

I hope you didn't skim over that statement, for it captures the heart of Christian faith and every person's story. You are God's kid!

J. I. Packer asserts, "You sum up the whole of New Testament teaching in a single phrase, if you speak of it as a revelation of the Fatherhood of the holy Creator. In the same way, you sum up the whole of New Testament religion if you describe it as the knowledge of God as one's holy Father. If you want to judge how well a person understands Christianity, find out how much he makes of the thought of being God's child, and having God as his Father. If this is not the thought that prompts and controls his worship and prayers and his whole outlook on life, it means that he does not understand Christianity very well at all."[2]

The heavenly Father treasures you as one of His own. You are not an orphan, even though you may sometimes feel alone.

"'I will be a Father to you, and you will be my sons and daughters,' says the Lord Almighty" (2 Cor. 6:18).

As I write this I am on a sabbatical, holed up in a cheap hotel in Dry Ridge, Kentucky. It's my birthday, and I miss my family. Softening the sting is the card my 16-year-old daughter, Lindsey, packed in my suitcase.

She begins, "Dear Dad, I am so happy that you are my 51-year-old dad and that you have been there for me for 51 years. You're the best, and I love you so much it's ridiculous. Reading *Diaper University* this semester has shown me just how lucky I am to have someone like you in my life."

Let me stop there. This is the first I've heard that Lindsey read *Diaper University,* and the news of that brought me a few happy tears. Shortly after her birth I wrote that book as my bumbling attempt to capture the emotion of a becoming a dad. Never had I imagined that such profound feelings were possible.

Upon returning from the hospital, I sat down and wrote: "We were more than delighted to exchange our come-as-you-want-and-go-as-you-please lifestyle for a stay-at-home-and-don't-dare-do-anything-else-such-as-eat-sleep-or-potty existence. Crying replaced quiet, singing lullabies replaced sleep, diapers replaced television—and we couldn't have dreamed up a better deal.

"Daddyhood is the greatest invention. Even better than the lava lamp. Don't ask me how, but I found myself transformed overnight into your typical father.

"You know the dad I'm talking about, don't you? He shoves a thousand baby pictures down your throat and demands, 'Look at this kid. Is this kid beautiful or, is this kid beautiful?'

"Suppose you want to tell the truth? 'No, that kid there is ugly. He's 1 hour old, he's missing his hair, and he has green veins in his nose. Now put away the picture so I can finish my sandwich.'

"You can say it, but no father will hear you. To Dad, the kid is perfect. Why? Because the baby is his. His blood. His flesh. His spine. His legacy. Why, the boy's a spitting miniature of his dad. And nothing can alter that daddy's love for his kid.

"At last I'm catching a glimpse of the way our Father sees us. Beyond crazy over us, He's so in love with us He would sacrifice anything to be with us.

"Why does He love us? Because we are His. His face. His hands. His legacy. We were created in His image. And nothing can alter our Daddy's love for His kids.

"Yes, I'm beginning to understand God's love for us. I think about it all night long."[3]

I'm glad Lindsey read that book. I want her to know how much I love her. I'm crazy about my kids and just don't have words to express my love adequately.

Who You Are Not

Now, if God calls me His kid, I gotta believe that He's crazy about me. He loves me even more than I do my girls—if that's even possible. The most important priority in His life is to have a relationship with me. So to define my identity through my Father's love is to reinforce the truth about who I am—and equally as important, who I am not.

I am not a useless speck of dust or a cosmic long shot. Nor am I just a number in some heavenly Apple computer (I'm assuming they're all using Macs up there).

Ellen White reminds us: "The perfection of God's work is as clearly seen in the tiniest insect as in the king of birds. The soul of the little child that believes in Christ is as precious in His sight as are the angels about His throne."[4] Did you catch that? God's perfect handiwork is evident in the tiniest insect—even in every ant! How much more, then, can we feel assured that our heavenly Father knows and loves every one of His kids?

You matter to God. He knows you. He treasures you. Make no mistake: before you were conceived by your earthly parents, you were conceived in the heart of your Father in heaven!

That's our memoir, published in the courts of heaven. Six words: "Not an accident; God's cherished child."

[1] http://en.wikipedia.org/wiki/Six-Word_Memoirs (accessed Feb. 29, 2012).

[2] J. I. Packer, *Knowing God* (Downers Grove, Ill.: InterVarsity Press, 1993), p. 182.

[3] Karl Haffner, *Diaper University* (Hagerstown, Md.: Review and Herald Pub. Assn., 1999), pp. 17, 18.

[4] Ellen G. White, *Counsels on Health* (Mountain View, Calif.: Pacific Press Pub. Assn., 1951), p. 419.

Saint Me:
I Am a Saint

As you ponder our question "Who am I?" does the word "saint" come to mind? It should. After all, if you are in Christ, you are a saint. Sainthood is an integral part of your identity.

The apostle Paul recognized as much when he addressed fellow believers. Note his salutations:

"Paul, an apostle of Jesus Christ by the will of God, to the *saints* who are in Ephesus, and faithful in Christ Jesus" (Eph. 1:1, NKJV).

"To the church of God which is at Corinth, to those who are sanctified in Christ Jesus, called *to be saints*" (1 Cor. 1:2, NKJV).

"Paul and Timothy, bondservants of Jesus Christ, To all the *saints* in Christ Jesus who are in Philippi" (Phil. 1:1, NKJV).

Clearly, Paul did not shy away from the S word. So why do we?

I think I know the answer. It's the pride, envy, gluttony, lust, anger, greed, sloth—that is, it's the seven (times 70!) sins in your life, isn't it?

It's hard to hang a halo on someone who acts like a demon. I can't say I encourage my parishioners to call me "Saint Karl." After 25 years in ministry, I still cringe at the sound of "*Elder* Haffner." The "elder" bit makes me sound so old and holy and perfect—so much like everything I don't feel that I am.

But the Bible calls me a saint. So why can't I believe it?

Sinner or Saint?

You simply can't claim to believe what Scripture teaches about your identity and dodge the saintly status. According to the Bible, you are a saint. That said, it's time to face this inconvenient truth: You are also a sinner.

Now, I am not suggesting that you are part saint, part sinner. Nope. You are 100 percent saint. And you are 100 percent sinner. Both. You recognize this tension in your soul, right?

Country singer Waylon Jennings expressed the angst when he described himself in "The Gemini Song" as both good and bad, with two sides that aren't friends with each other.[1]

Jumping to another musical genre, we get the same story. Some years ago *Time* magazine interviewed Kanye West, former rap artist of the year and nominated for 30 Grammys. One of his best-known songs is called "Jesus Walks." It's a hip-hop prayer asking God to walk closely with him.

The interviewer asked West, "What do you say to people who see a contradiction between the devoutness of your Grammy-nominated hit 'Jesus Walks' and the profanity and sexual content on the rest of your album?"

West replied, "It's definitely a contradiction. Contradiction is part of who everybody is. I am a real person, and I make my mistakes and I laugh and I cry and I smile and I hate and I love. One song is 'I love God,' and the next song is 'Can you come over?' That's how I feel. Sometimes you're in church, and you're looking at the girl's dress right next to you."[2]

West is spot on, isn't he? Seneca, the Roman philosopher, said it this way:

"People love their vices and hate them at the same time; they hate their sins and cannot leave them."

The same Abraham who would sacrifice his son to God also lied to Pharaoh, claiming his wife to be his sister. The David who penned many psalms also committed adultery and murder. And the same Peter who confessed Jesus as the Messiah went on to deny Him three times. It's the human story for all of us: sinner *and* saint.

Paul describes our struggle: "I do not understand what I do. For what I want to do I do not do, but what I hate I do" (Rom. 7:15).

Can you relate?

In Galatians 5:17 the apostle portrayed our predicament: "For the flesh desires what is contrary to the Spirit, and the Spirit what is contrary to the flesh. They are in conflict with each other, so that you are not to do whatever you want."

In the words of Carl Sandburg: "There is an eagle in me that wants to soar, and there is a hippopotamus in me that wants to wallow in the mud."[3]

Who am I? I am an eagle. I am a hippopotamus. For my Facebook status, I think that qualifies as "It's complicated." So let's dissect it.

100 Percent Sinner

First, let's think about our status as sinners. Paul tells us in Romans

5:12 that "sin entered the world through one man, and death through sin, and in this way death came to all people, because all sinned."

Any questions? All have "sinned and fallen short of the glory of God" (Rom. 3:23). Tracing back to Adam and Eve, every one of us was born a full-out, 100 percent, bona fide sinner.

You probably remember the horrific news of April 20, 1999, about Columbine High School. Dylan Klebold and Eric Harris killed 12 students and one teacher, and injured 24 others before claiming their own lives. On the tenth anniversary of the tragedy Dylan Klebold's mother, Susan Klebold, reflected in *Oprah* magazine:

"In raising Dylan, I taught him how to protect himself from a host of dangers: lightning, snakebites, head injuries, skin cancer, smoking, drinking, sexually transmitted diseases, drug addiction, reckless driving, even carbon monoxide poisoning. It never occurred to me that the gravest danger—to him and, as it turned out, to many others—might come from within."[4]

Such a sinner resides in every human being.

100 Percent Saint

Now let's think about our status as saints.

In our day the word "saint" conjures up images of hyper-holy people complete with halos. In the New Testament, however, "saint" literally meant "holy one." The designation of "saint" spoke to a person's position, not to his or her moral behavior. In other words, saints are not perfect people. Rather, they are imperfect people who enjoy a new and secure position in Christ. Paul says, "Therefore, if anyone is in Christ, the new creation has come: The old has gone, the new is here!" (2 Cor. 5:17).

Sainthood speaks to a sinner's standing relative to Christ. Klyne Snodgrass, professor of New Testament studies at North Park Theological Seminary in Chicago, explains it this way:

"The word *holy* describes something separated or set apart. God is holy because He is separated from humans. He cannot be grouped with them as the same kind of being. Paul refers to the Corinthians as 'sanctified in Christ Jesus, called to be saints' (1 Corinthians 1:2). People who are *sanctified* are those who have been set apart by God, even if they are not living holy lives as they should (which was definitely true of the Corinthian church)."[5]

You see, the point of the word "saints" is to emphasize that God has separated us to Himself and has given us a new standing in Christ.

This is what happens in a marriage. That union between a man and a woman is set apart—sanctified by God. It is made holy. When I mess up in my marriage, it doesn't change my status as Cherié's husband. If it did, then my marriage would have gone kaput within the first month.

No sooner did we return from the honeymoon than Cherié and I had our first big squabble. I demanded that we purchase a used ski boat. She insisted that a boat could wait. We needed dinnerware.

"We can use paper plates," I said.

"But we don't *need* a boat," she countered.

So we compromised. I bought the boat, and we used paper plates. OK, I guess that's not much of a compromise.

As it turns out, that was one of my more spectacular "bonehead" moves. In the first week of boat ownership, tragedy struck. An unseasonably heavy rainfall filled the boat with water, and it sank to the bottom of Lake Chapin. For the next year we commemorated the drowning at every meal (when we ate on paper plates). The end.

It was the end of the boat, but not the end of my status as a husband. Believe it or not, 26 years later we're still blissfully, deliriously happily married in a fairytale nirvana. Well, OK, let's just say we're definitely still married. Even though I have demonstrated a stunning capacity to be a real jerk, my behavior has not changed my standing as a husband. I could hoard the M&Ms, be short-tempered with my kids, criticize my wife's cooking, and still be Cherié's husband. Why? Because God set our relationship apart; He made it holy.

In the same way, God has separated us to Himself. Consequently, our status as saints is secure because of our standing with Christ. Sainthood is about our position in relation to Jesus—not about our perfect behavior. In this way we are both sinner and saint, both Judas and Jesus.

Judas or Jesus? Yes.

In his fictional book *Sophia House* author Michael O'Brien tells the story of a famous young painter hired during the Middle Ages to create a mural depicting the life of Christ for a prominent church in Paris. For years the artist labored, and his mural became known as the marvel of its time. Yet it was not finished. Somehow he couldn't complete two of the faces— the Christ child and Judas Iscariot. Whenever he tried to paint the empty spaces, he felt frustrated and disappointed at the results.

He prayed for inspiration. Finally, a breakthrough: he happened upon a group of children playing. Among them was a boy who had the face of an angel and who radiated righteousness. The artist invited him to sit as a model of the Christ child. With his parents' permission the child obliged, and the final portrait was perfect.

Yet the painter still had an empty space on his mural. He could not find the right model for the face of Judas. Many wannabe models volunteered. Some posers did indeed possess wicked, deformed, or corrupt faces, but to the artist, none of them seemed quite right. He wanted a face so twisted and ruined by its surrender to depravity that all who gazed upon it would see Satan in human flesh.

Many years passed. The artist often retreated to the church to pray for inspiration. Although he longed to complete his project, a part of him secretly hoped the face of Judas would forever elude him. It was an unsettling thought that he should meet a human soul so sinister that he would look like the artist's concept of sin incarnate.

Then one afternoon, as he sat in the church, a beggar staggered down the aisle and knelt at the steps of the altar. He reeked of cheap wine, and his tattered clothing hung from his haggard figure. Although not an old man, he was hunched over as if weighted by an immense burden of dark memories. His face, however, was perfect! Perfectly evil, that is. The artist took the broken man home with him, fed him, washed his diseased flesh, clothed him and spoke to him warmly, as if with a friend. He instructed his children to treat the visitor with the greatest respect. His wife, a kind and devout woman, prepared fine meals for him. But the poor man dwelt in their midst as if made of stone.

He was, however, willing to pose for the mural. Weeks went by, and as the work progressed, the beggar would look from time to time at the image of himself coming to life on the canvas. A curious grief and horror would fill his eyes. One day, seeing the model's distress, the artist paused in his labor, laying down his brush.

"My friend," he said, "your heart is troubled. What is it?"

Turning his face, the man's eyes puddled with tears. Finally, he asked, "Do you not remember me? Years ago I was your model for the Christ child."

It is your story, and it is my story. We are both Judas and Jesus wrapped up into one person—both sinner and saint.

In the words of Martin Luther, *simul iustus et peccator*, which means "at the same time, saint and sinner." Luther was not saying that we are sometimes one and then the other. We are saint and sinner *at the same time*.

Even when we are performing the most sacred act, we do so as sinners. And when we are guilty of sin, we are still saints.

Aleksandr Solzhenitsyn observed, "If only there were evil people somewhere insidiously committing evil deeds, and it were necessary only to separate them from the rest of us and destroy them. But the line dividing good and evil cuts through the heart of every human being. And who is willing to destroy a piece of his own heart?"[6]

You cannot extract the Judas without removing the Jesus. Nor can you take out the Jesus without extracting the Judas. Both live in every human heart.

At this point it becomes a matter of perspective. If in fact you are both Judas and Jesus, sinner and saint, do you see yourself as a sinner who does his or her best to become a saint? Or do you view yourself as a saint who occasionally sins? Clarity on this issue is critical.

A Sinner Striving for Sainthood

If you perceive yourself as a sinner trying your best to be a saint, you will always feel frustrated. Listen to Paul's insight:

"Have some of you noticed that we are not yet perfect? (No great surprise, right?) And are you ready to make the accusation that since people like me, who go through Christ in order to get things right with God, aren't perfectly virtuous, Christ must therefore be an accessory to sin? The accusation is frivolous. If I was 'trying to be good,' I would be rebuilding the same old barn that I tore down. I would be acting as a charlatan" (Gal. 2:17, 18, Message).

When we see ourselves as sinners who need to work hard to become saints, it's like tearing out the old carpet in your family room and then re-installing it. Do that, and don't be surprised if your friends call you a kook. When we try to remove the old sins and in our own strength attempt to replace our sin with sainthood, it's just as kooky.

Scholars Bill Thrall and Bruce McNicol put it like this:

"Many of us have spent too much of our lives serving God while embracing a theology of 'rebuilding the same old barn.' . . . We have placed all our efforts in 'trying to be good.' Yet we are broken, defeated, lonely, and despairing. . . . In this life, we who have trusted Christ will always have these two constants: our sin issues and our new identity."[7]

A Saint Who Stumbles in Sin

So you can slave away on your sin issues and try to become a saint.

Or you can see yourself as a saint because of your standing in Christ. The Bible clarifies your identity: You are not a sinner trying to be a saint, but a saint who occasionally sins. That means you trust God and believe that when He claims you are righteous, His perfect child, you are in fact just that—a saint.

Listen to how Paul goes on to unpack the concept:

"What actually took place is this: I tried keeping rules and working my head off to please God, and it didn't work. So I quit being a 'law man' so that I could be God's man. Christ's life showed me how, and enabled me to do it. I identified myself completely with him. Indeed, I have been crucified with Christ. My ego is no longer central. It is no longer important that I appear righteous before you or have your good opinion, and I am no longer driven to impress God. Christ lives in me. The life you see me living is not 'mine,' but it is lived by faith in the Son of God, who loved me and gave himself for me. I am not going to go back on that" (verses 19, 20, Message).

Bill Thrall and Bruce McNicol offer this commentary:

"When Christians see themselves as [sinners trying to be good] they have no choice but to live life as sinners, strenuously striving to become saints. Naturally, this effort leads to failure because we're not in charge of our sainthood. Our sainthood has already been accomplished by our loving Savior, Jesus Christ. Therefore, when Christians are able to see themselves as 'saints who sin,' as Christ-in-me creatures, as clothed with robes of righteousness, they have the only basis to grow up into what is already true of them. God says we are righteous, and this becomes the context or the condition that allows Christ to dwell in us. If my vision of what I can become is based on my vision of who Jesus says I already am— righteous—I can relax and mature into something I already am. When we trust God, . . . our self-identity builds on His assessment, not ours—on His righteousness, not our own 'righteousness.'"[8]

So the bottom line is that I am not a sinner trying to change myself into a saint. No! I am a saint in Christ, who stumbles (a lot!), but that does not change my identity as righteous in Him.

The caterpillar provides a picture of this. Present a caterpillar to a biologist and ask him to inspect its DNA. "I realize this looks like a caterpillar," he would say, "but scientifically, according to every test— including DNA—this is fully and completely a butterfly." God designed the creature to look nothing like a butterfly. But regardless of the external attributes, it is in fact a perfectly complete butterfly. That is its identity.

Since the caterpillar is a butterfly, one day it will display butterfly behavior. The caterpillar matures into what is already true about it. Meanwhile, scolding the caterpillar for not acting more butterfly-like is like bawling out the kindergarten basketball team in the Midget League for not dunking.

The soaring will come. It is in our DNA. We are godly saints, righteous in Christ. And we can't make ourselves more righteous than we already are. Thus God views us through the lens of what He knows to be true about us—namely that we *are* saints. Our job is not necessarily to work on cleaning up our sins. Rather, it is to live in Christ and trust in what He says about who we are in Him.

We are not sinners trying to be saints. We are saints who sin whenever we stop trusting Jesus.

---

[1] www.metrolyrics.com/gemini-song-when-im-bad-im-bad-lyrics-waylon-jennings. html (accessed Mar. 1, 2012).

[2] Barbara Kiviat, "10 Questions for Kanye West," *Time,* Dec. 17, 2004, www.time. com/time/magazine/article/0,9171,1009743,00.html (accessed Mar. 1, 2012).

[3] http://thinkexist.com/quotation/there_is_an_eagle_in_me_that_wants_to_soar-and/192933.html (accessed Mar. 1, 2012).

[4] Susan Klebold, "I Will Never Know Why," *Oprah,* November 2009, www.oprah. com/world/Susan-Klebolds-O-Magazine-Essay-I-Will-Never-Know-Why/7 (accessed Mar. 1, 2012).

[5] www.vop.com/daily_archive.php?date=2008-05-08 (accessed Apr. 2, 2012).

[6] www.goodreads.com/author/quotes/10420.Aleksandr_I_Solzhenitsyn (accessed Mar. 2, 2012).

[7] Bill Thrall and Bruce McNicol, "Chapter Two: Communities of Grace," in Alan Andrews, ed., *The Kingdom Life* (Colorado Springs, Colo.: NavPress, 2010), p. 72.

[8] *Ibid.*, p. 71.

Dual Citizenship:
I Am a Colonist

In October 2005 native Kenyan Moses Bittok took the oath of U.S. citizenship at the federal building in Des Moines, Iowa. He officially became an American, and that alone made it the happiest day of his life. But on that day there was even more good news.

On the way home Bittok stopped at a gas station to check the winning numbers in Iowa's Hot Lotto Game. Now his good fortune also included a $1.89 million jackpot!

"It's almost like you adopted a new country and then they netted you $1.8 million," Bittok said. "It doesn't happen anywhere—I guess only in America."[1]

Similarly, new life in Christ gives us citizenship into the kingdom of God. But the good news doesn't stop there. Yes, we will hold a deed to a mansion on Golden Avenue someday, but it encompasses so much more. It has major implications for understanding our identity and how we live today.

Often our identity is entwined in our heritage and where we live. Ask someone to finish the sentence "I am a . . ." and you're likely to hear "I am an American" or "I am a Canadian" or "I am a New Yorker"—something like that. But to limit our identity to our current address is shortsighted and, well, not biblical.

Paul makes it clear that for believers, our citizenship is in heaven:

"For, as I have often told you before and now tell you again even with tears, many live as enemies of the cross of Christ. Their destiny is destruction, their god is their stomach, and their glory is in their shame. Their mind is set on earthly things. But our citizenship is in heaven" (Phil. 3:18-20).

Paul warns us not to align ourselves too closely with our earthly connections. Our strongest affiliation is with heaven, which is our destiny. And in contrast, for the people of the world, "their destiny is destruction."

Seeing Blind

English author H. G. Wells is famous for such science fiction novels as *The Time Machine, The Invisible Man,* and *The War of the Worlds.* He also wrote a short story called "The Country of the Blind." As the title suggests, it's about an inaccessible, lush valley in Ecuador where a strange disease has rendered everyone blind. For many generations citizens of this region had no recollection of sight, color, or the outside world at all. Finally a foreigner named Nunez literally fell into their midst. After falling from a high cliff, he staggered into the forgotten community. At last they had somebody in their midst who could see!

Realizing that everyone else was blind, Nunez reveled in the old cliché "In the country of the blind, the one-eyed man is king." Wells writes:

"He tried at first on several occasions to tell them of sight. 'Look you here, you people,' he said, 'there are things you do not understand in me.'

"Once or twice one or two of them attended to him; they sat with faces downcast and ears turned intelligently toward him, and he did his best to tell them what it was to see."[2]

But they never believed him. Instead, they assumed he was crazy.

The story heats up when Nunez falls in love with a girl there. It disconcerted the girl's father, Yacob, who went to a doctor to discuss his apprehensions about his daughter's suitor. The doctor explained:

"'Those queer things that are called the eyes, and which exist to make an agreeable depression in the face, are diseased, in the case of Nunez, in such a way as to affect his brain. They are greatly distended, he has eyelashes, and his eyelids move, and consequently his brain is in a state of constant irritation and distraction.'

"'Yes?' said old Yacob. 'Yes?'

"'And I think I may say with reasonable certainty that in order to cure him complete, all that we need to do is a simple and easy surgical operation—namely, to remove these irritant bodies.'

"'And then he will be sane?'

"'Then he will be perfectly sane, and a quite admirable citizen.'

"'Thank Heaven for science!' said old Yacob, and went forth at once to tell Nunez of his happy hopes."[3]

Nunez would not be allowed to marry Yacob's daughter unless he submitted to an operation that would blind him. So what would he do? Wells writes:

"He walked away.

"He had fully meant to go to a lonely place where the meadows were beautiful with white narcissus, and there remain until the hour of his sacrifice should come, but as he walked he lifted up his eyes and saw the morning, the morning like an angel in golden armour, marching down the steeps. . . .

"It seemed to him that before this splendour, he and this blind world in the valley, and his love and all, were no more than a pit of sin."[4]

So the man who could see escaped the country of the blind with his life. He would not remain in the pit of sin.

We too live in a world of the blind—a world proud of its science, sure of its health, oblivious to the light. Not only is it pitiful, it is deadly. Remember, "their destiny is destruction" (Phil. 3:19).

Living Light

Jesus refers to "the country of the blind" as "the world." He explained, "Light has come into the world, but people loved darkness instead of light because their deeds were evil" (John 3:19). In His last words to His disciples before going to the cross, Jesus warned them of the hostility they would face—just as He had—in this country of the blind. Yet rather than pulling His beloved followers *out* of this hostile world, Jesus sent His own Spirit into His people to convince this world of its blindness.

Jesus prayed for this to happen. Listen to His heart cry:

"I will remain in the world no longer, but they are still in the world, and I am coming to you. Holy Father, protect them by the power of your name, the name you gave me, so that they may be one as we are one. While I was with them, I protected them and kept them safe by that name you gave me. None has been lost except the one doomed to destruction so that Scripture would be fulfilled.

"I am coming to you now, but I say these things while I am still in the world, so that they may have the full measure of my joy within them. I have given them your word and the world has hated them, for they are not of the world any more than I am of the world. My prayer is not that you take them out of the world but that you protect them from the evil one. They are not of the world, even as I am not of it" (John 17:11-16).

Notice that Jesus specifically states that His prayer is *not* that you and I be taken out of this blind and evil world of darkness. Rather, He prays for our protection. While we are citizens of His kingdom, we are not home—not yet. We are backpacking through our world to a better one.

A story tells of a man who was traveling through Europe. He happened upon a town in which there lived a very well-known kabbalist. Knowing his time in the town would be very short, the traveler went straight to the kabbalist. When the traveler entered the house of the great mystical sage, he was confounded. It contained nothing more than a table, a bed, and some books.

He asked in amazement, "This is all you have here? How do you live like this?"

The kabbalist replied, "What about you? All you have is those few things that are in your bag."

"Yes," the traveler explained, "but I am only on a journey, temporarily passing through."

"I am also only on a journey, temporarily passing through," the kabbalist replied.

Thinking Colony

James Moffatt's paraphrase of Philippians renders Paul's statement that we are citizens of heaven in this way: "But we are a colony of heaven" (Phil. 3:20, Moffatt).

Think about the implications. What is a colony? Dictionary.com answers:

"A group of people who leave their native country to form in a new land a settlement subject to, or connected with, the parent nation."

You see, even though colonists may settle in a distant, often hostile place, they still live under the control of and in accordance with the shared values of their home country.

Lindsey Garmon explains: "Clearly, a colony is an extension or outpost of one culture in the midst of another. For Christians, heaven is our homeland—our dominant culture. Temporarily, we are residents of the distant, and sometimes hostile, setting of this earth. Yet, as 'citizens of heaven' and members of 'a heavenly colony,' we continually seek to faithfully present and preserve the holy culture of heaven in the midst of the unholy culture of earth."[5]

Being a citizen of heaven does not necessarily call for isolation from the world. There is, and always has been, a flavor of faith that calls for complete segregation from the world for fear that worldly values will corrupt. The ancient community at Qumran—from which we received the Dead Sea scrolls—is an example of people who shunned the world. They went so far as to move out into the desert and establish an independent community. Monasteries and convents sometimes embrace the same fear of the world.

Simeon the Stylite is an example of someone who viewed his citizenship in heaven as a command to avoid all things worldly. He lived around A.D. 400 in northern Syria. The tag of "stylite" comes from the Greek word *style*, meaning "pillar." After working as a shepherd boy, he entered a monastery at the age of 15.

Wikipedia.com records the occasion when "[Simeon] commenced a severe regimen of fasting for Lent and was visited by the head of the monastery, who left him some water and loaves. A number of days later, Simeon was discovered unconscious, with the water and loaves untouched. When he was brought back to the monastery, it was discovered that he had bound his waist with a girdle made of palm fronds so tightly that days of soaking were required to remove the fibres from the wound formed."[6]

And what happened to Simeon for his super-holy behavior? He got booted out of the monastery. But that suited him fine, because even the monastery was too worldly for his liking.

To escape from the world, Simeon perched himself on top of a 45-foot pillar in the middle of the desert. People were so impressed by his austerity that they sought him out and would congregate around his pillar to listen to his teaching.

After 36 years on his pillar, Simeon died on September 2, 459. He inspired many imitators, and for the next century, ascetics living on pillars were a common sight throughout the Byzantine Levant, although few managed to survive as long as Simeon. As bizarre as the story seems, scholars do not question the historicity of Simeon the Stylite.

Where Shall We Then Live?

So is this what God had in mind when He taught that we are not citizens of this world, only pilgrims passing through? Should we move to Tristan de Cunha, the spot ranked number one of the "Top 10 Most Remote Places in the World"? It is an archipelago of small islands located in the southern Atlantic Ocean. The nearest land to the island is South Africa, roughly 1,700 miles away, while the South American coast lies at a distance of about 2,000 miles.[7] It might have a pillar on which I could perch for the next 36 years. You reckon that's a good plan?

Obviously our identity as citizens of heaven does not mean that we are to spurn the world around us. On the contrary, as we will explore in the next section, understanding who we are in Christ is our impetus to charge into the world and fulfill our God-ordained destiny.

Jesus asserts, "You are the light of the world. A town built on a hill cannot be hidden. Neither do people light a lamp and put it under a bowl. Instead they put it on its stand, and it gives light to everyone in the house. In the same way, let your light shine before others, that they may see your good deeds and glorify your Father in heaven" (Matt. 5:14-16).

Jesus affirms our identity as citizens of heaven that are on a mission to shine God's light in this dark place. As we do so, it does not compromise our identity but rather confirms it.

During the Vietnam War a man named A. J. Muste stood in front of the White House with a candle night after night. One cold and rainy night he stood there alone. A reporter asked him, "Mr. Muste, do you really think you are going to change the policies of this country by standing out here alone at night with a candle?"

"Oh no," Muste replied, "I don't do it to change the country. I do it so the country won't change me."

When we respond to God's calling and live as light-bearing citizens of His kingdom, we stand uncompromising in our conviction. Ironically, by doing it, we safeguard our souls against the world changing us. We enjoy laserlike clarity about who we are and whom God made us to be. Thus we serve Him as His light in a dark world—not just to transform the world, but also so the world won't change us.

The Epistle to Diognetus described Christians resolute in their dual citizenship:

"Their lot is cast 'in the flesh,' but they do not live 'after the flesh.' They pass their time upon the earth, but they have their citizenship in heaven. They obey the appointed laws, and they surpass the laws in their own lives. They love all men and are persecuted by all men. They are unknown and they are condemned. They are put to death and they gain life. 'They are poor and make many rich'; they lack all things and have all things in abundance. . . . To put it shortly, what the soul is in the body, that the Christians are in the world."[8]

---

[1] www.powerball.com/hotlotto/winners/2005/092105ia.shtml (accessed Mar. 2, 2012).
[2] H. G. Wells, "The Country of the Blind," www.online-literature.com/wellshg/3/ (accessed Mar. 3, 2012).
[3] *Ibid.*

[4] *Ibid.*

[5] Lindsey Garmon, *Citizens of Heaven—Residents of Earth* (21st Century Christian, 2010), http://21stcc.com/pdfs/samplepages/9780890985472.pdf (accessed Mar. 3, 2012).

[6] http://en.wikipedia.org/wiki/Simeon_Stylites (accessed Mar. 3, 2012).

[7] "Top 10 Most Remote Places in the World," www.toptenz.net/top-10-most-remote-places-on-planet-earth.php#ixzzlo3wPjaD3 (accessed Mar. 3, 2012).

[8] *The Epistle to Diognetus* V-VI (c. A.D. 130-200), http://garynebeker.blogspot.com/2007/05/quote-of-month-for-distinction-between.html (accessed Mar. 3, 2012).

Why **Am I Here?**

*"You are not here merely to make a living.
You are here in order to enable the world to live more amply,
with greater vision, with a finer spirit of hope and achievement.
You are here to enrich the world,
and you impoverish yourself if you forget the errand."*

—anonymous

*"Why am I here?
I want answers now, or I want them eventually!"*

—Homer Simpson

*"When I stand before God at the end of my life,
I would hope that I would not have a single bit of talent left,
and could say, 'I used everything you gave me.'"*

—Erma Bombeck

"The purpose of life is a life of purpose."

—Robert Byrne

*"Here is the test to find whether your mission on earth is finished.
If you're alive, it isn't."*

—Richard Bach

Existential Answers From Einstein, Tutu, Pinocchio . . .

When were you born? Easy answer, right? I was born on February 22. That means I share a birthday with George Washington, Drew Barrymore, Ted Kennedy, Robert Kardashian, and Vijay Singh.

Another question: Where were you born? Again, I don't have to think to answer. I was born in Plentywood, Montana, population: 1,734. As the story goes, many years ago a group of cowboys watched in exasperation as a chuck wagon cook attempted to start a fire with damp buffalo chips. Finally, in frustration, the notorious Dutch Henry said, "If you'll go two miles up this creek, you'll find plenty wood." You'll also find my birthplace.

But now for a stickier question: *Why* were you born? You can't get this answer from a birth certificate. An alarm clock can tell you *when* to get out of bed, but it won't tell you *why* to get up. *Why* were you born?

While it's important to understand who we are—God's children, saints, and citizens of His kingdom—we must graduate to a deeper question: Why are we here?

Wispily Speaking

Frankly, we don't have much time to figure it out. It hit me with fresh force the other day when a disturbing thought assaulted me. Reflecting on my recent passage into the sixth decade of life, it dawned on me that when my daughter, Claire, reaches this same milestone and celebrates her fiftieth birthday, I will be 90! I probably won't be scampering around, blasting a squawker blowout at that party. I'm still depressed by the thought. How is it that life evaporates so quickly?

The Bible says, "You're nothing but a wisp of fog, catching a brief bit of sun before disappearing" (James 4:14, Message). The psalmist reminds us, "Surely every man is a mere breath" (Ps. 39:11, NASB). Compared to God and eternity, your life is a blink; a heartbeat; a breath. Your life is over faster than you can ask, "Why am I here?"

Of course, our perspective on time is very different from God's. For example, consider a recent tennis tournament for super seniors—people 90 and above. In the finals, a 92-year-old competed against a 94-year-old. During the match the younger athlete cracked a crosscourt forehand, and the 94-year-old couldn't chase it down. Dropping his racquet in disgust, he stood up straight and sighed, "Oooooooh . . . to be 92 again!"

For us, a couple years may feel like a long time; a big deal. With God, 100 years is a baby step in an infinite number of hikes around the world.

We don't have much time to figure out the answer. So why are we here?

Googling that question took me to an online quiz that promised to give me my answer. Indulging my writer's block, I started clicking away, and sure enough, in short order I had an answer. According to the Internet, 85 percent of me is here "to love." The next-highest answer tells me that 80 percent of me is here "to entertain." At the bottom of my list is the calling "to shine" (40 percent). That's not all that helpful . . .

Meaningwise

When it comes to the big questions—Why am I here? What is my destiny? What is the meaning of life?—there are no simple answers.

One study, conducted by four psychologists, compiled quotations from famous people about the meaning of life. Analyzing the quotes from 195 men and women who lived within the past few centuries, they categorized their findings into eight general answers:

1. *Life is primarily to be enjoyed and experienced. Enjoy the moment and the journey.* It was the top answer—17 percent embraced this worldview (Ralph Waldo Emerson, Cary Grant, Janis Joplin, and Sinclair Lewis). As Janis Joplin sang, "You got to get it while you can."

2. *We live to express compassion to others, to love, to serve.* Thirteen percent endorsed this theme (Albert Einstein, Mohandas Gandhi, and the Dalai Lama). Albert Einstein said, "Only a life lived for others is a life worthwhile."

3. *Life is unknowable; a mystery.* Thirteen percent agreed with this idea (Albert Camus, Bob Dylan, and Stephen Hawking). Hawking wrote that if we discover the answer to why we are here, "it would be the ultimate triumph of human reason—for then we would know the mind of God."

4. *Life has no meaning.* Eleven percent held to a futile notion of life (Sigmund Freud, Franz Kafka, Bertrand Russell, Jean-Paul Sartre, and Clarence Darrow). Darrow compared life to a ship that is "tossed by every wave and by every wind; a ship headed to no port and no harbor, with no rudder, no compass, no pilot, simply floating for a time, then lost in the waves." That's a cheery little quip, eh?

5. *We are to worship God and prepare for the afterlife.* Another 11 percent endorsed this theme (Desmond Tutu, Billy Graham, Martin Luther King, Jr., and Mother Teresa). Desmond Tutu said, "[We should] give God glory by reflecting His beauty and His love. That is why we are here, and that is the purpose of our lives."

6. *Life is a struggle.* Eight percent accepted a more fatalistic outlook (Charles Dickens, Benjamin Disraeli, and Jonathan Swift). Swift wrote that life is a "tragedy wherein we sit as spectators for a while and then act our part in it."

7. *We are to create our own meaning of life.* Five percent suggested that we've got to come up with our own meaning (Carl Sagan, Simone DeBeauvoir, and Carl Jung). Carl Sagan wrote: "We live in a vast and awesome universe in which, daily, suns are made and worlds destroyed, where humanity clings to an obscure clod of rock. The significance of our lives and our fragile realm derives from our own wisdom and courage. We are the custodians of life's meaning."

8. *Life is a joke.* Last, 4 percent adopted this theme (Albert Camus, Charlie Chaplin, Lou Reed, and Oscar Wilde). Charlie Chaplin described life as "a tragedy when seen in close-up but a comedy in the long shot." *

Which worldview would you embrace? If you accept the biblical answer to the question "Who am I?" then it definitely shapes your opinion on why you are here. Assuming that you are a beloved child of God, perfect in His righteousness, chosen and redeemed for an eternity in His presence, then you simply can't endorse most of these ideologies. Life is not a joke. Nor is it meaningless or simply a struggle or a mystery.

You are here for a reason. And what is it? A question this weighty deserves your most astute thinking . . . so let's consult Pinocchio.

Pondering With Pinocchio

The classic tale *Pinocchio,* set in the late 1800s, tells of Geppetto, an Italian woodcarver who creates a boy puppet named Pinocchio. When a fairy magically gives this puppet life, Geppetto is startled by what he sees in his shop. Let's eavesdrop on that first conversation:

"Who are you?" Geppetto asks Pinocchio.

"Well, you should know," the puppet replies. "You gave me my name. And now you don't even recognize me!"

"You are not real. It's just . . ." The woodcarver struggles to believe.

"Yes, I am! I am a real boy! Well, my heart is still made of wood, but when I hear it beat properly, then I'll be real! That's what the fairy said!"

"The fairy?" Geppetto asks. "You mean there's a fairy here, too?"

Pinocchio nods furiously.

"A wooden puppet comes to life—and now there's a fairy?" Overwhelmed, the man feels Pinocchio's arms and face to see if he is indeed a real "live" boy. Soon tears well up in his eyes. "You're alive! Do you understand? You're alive!"

"I'm alive!" Pinocchio repeats. Then a pensive look covers his face. "What do you mean 'I'm alive'?"

"What does it mean? Well, unless I'm going mad, and this isn't just a dream, it means you have a life to live."

"And what do you have a life for?" Pinocchio asks.

Unable to find an answer, Geppetto falls silent.

"And so is this a good thing or bad thing?" the former puppet wonders.

"No—it's a beautiful thing. A wonderful thing! What do you have it for? Uhhhhh . . . " Geppetto still has a puzzled look on his face. He concludes, "I'll have to think about it."

You, too, have a life to live. It's a beautiful thing; a wonderful thing. But what is your life for?

Think about it.

* Richard Kinnier, Jerry Kernes, Nancy Tribbensee, Christina Van Puymbroeck, in *Journal of Humanistic Psychology* 43, no. 1 (Winter 2003): 105-118.

A Mist Not to Be Missed

Bill Clinton was 30 when he was appointed attorney general of Arkansas. Two years later he was elected governor of Arkansas, making him the youngest person in the nation to hold such a high office. He was only 46 when he took over the oval office as president. For most of his life he has been thought of as "the young guy."

As he braced himself for his impending sixtieth birthday in August of 2006, however, a melancholy Clinton reluctantly admitted that life had changed. No longer the youthful saxophonist wailing away on MTV, the white-haired former president reflected:

"For most of my working life, I was the youngest person doing what I was doing. Then one day I woke up, and I was the oldest person in every room. In just a few days I will be 60 years old. I hate it, but it's true."[1]

As Phyllis Diller once quipped, "I don't know how you feel about old age . . . but in my case I didn't even see it coming. It hit me from the rear."

Yep, it slams into all of us. Given this reality, we would be wise to digest the counsel of James. In chapter 4 he makes four simple observations that are oh, so true.

1. You Cannot Presume Tomorrow

First, James reminds us that we cannot count on there always being a tomorrow. "Now listen, you who say, 'Today or tomorrow we will go to this or that city, spend a year there, carry on business and make money.' Why, you do not even know what will happen tomorrow" (James 4:13, 14).

You make your plans. You scheme to fatten your portfolio. You pursue your destiny of success.

"Not so fast," James would counsel. "First, take into consideration that you may not even be around tomorrow."

Mary Leonard of Louisville, Kentucky, heard that message loud and clear. For 11 years she dealt with polymyositis, a rare inflammatory tissue disease that invades the muscles. It has no known cause or cure. Her case turned deadly when the condition invaded her heart. In March of 2010 doctors delivered the grim news: "You have 24 to 48 hours to live."

But doctors are fallible. They don't know what will happen tomorrow, either. As Mary's story reminds us, they can be dead wrong—in a good sort of way.

After 20 days in a hospice center, another 51 days in rehabilitation, and some months at home, Mary was still alive. During that time she reflected often on the truism from James that we can't begin to presume tomorrow.

"I call myself an average Christian," she said. "I don't know exactly why God has done this for me, but I do know that life looks different now."

How did Mary's life change? She lived with a keen awareness that today could be her last day on this earth. Consequently, she was quick to share five life lessons she had learned through her ordeal:

1. Know that prayer is powerful.
2. Mend fences now.
3. Release the reins of life to God.
4. Know that God is able—more than able.
5. Put your focus on what really matters.[2]

I thought of her last point when I got this tweet today from Bob Goff: "I used to be afraid that I'd fail at things that mattered; now I'm concerned that I'll succeed at things that don't."

I reckon James would appreciate Mary's perspective. We have no guarantee for tomorrow, so make today count.

2. Life Is a Mist

Second, James points out that life is fleeting. He writes:

"What is your life? You are a mist that appears for a little while and then vanishes" (James 4:14).

I sure don't like it, but I know he is right. Life whizzes by us with alarming speed. I can see that clearly . . . in others. I notice the receding hairline, the new glasses, the slowed step, the faltering memory, the wrinkles, the pudgy waistline—all the telltale signs of aging are really obvious to me when I look at others. But me? I don't feel any older than when I wrote my first book (18 years ago!).

I can relate to the woman who moved to a new town and was waiting for her first appointment with a new dentist. She noticed his D.D.S. diploma, which bore his full name. Suddenly she remembered a tall, handsome, dark-haired boy with the same name from her high school class, years before. *Could this be the heartthrob I had a crush on way back then?* She indulged her furtive memories as she recounted how chiseled, athletic, and smart he had been.

Upon meeting the dentist, she quickly dismissed any notion that the man was the same guy. He was bald, fat, and way too old to be her classmate. But the more they talked, the more she wondered. Finally she just asked him.

"You didn't by chance go to Morgan Park High School, did you?"

"Yes!" he exclaimed. "I'm a Mustang."

"Really?" she gasped in disbelief. "When did you graduate?"

"Class of 1959."

"Really? You were in my class!" she squealed.

"Really?" he said, looking at her closely. "What subject did you teach?"

We're quick to notice the effects of aging in others . . . but in ourselves? As Morrie Venden used to say: "At my class reunions anymore my old classmates are all so bald and fat they don't recognize me."

I get that. Life is a mist. If you want to fulfill your destiny and put a dent in this world, you've got only today. Hurry up. It's over as quickly as fog evaporates.

After living in Walla Walla, Washington, for 10 years, we accepted a call to pastor in Ohio. We moved into transitional housing while I returned by myself to meet the movers and pack up the van heading east.

The day was a tornado of activity—cleaning, packing, hauling. It offered no time for glum reflection. Our junk needed to get in the truck.

But then the movers disappeared for the night. I was alone. Suddenly an avalanche of memories overwhelmed me, sparked by a few lines on the back of a door. Next to each line was a date. The dates marked a decade of growth for our girls.

I stared at the mark recording Lindsey's height when we moved into the house. It just eclipsed my knee. Lindsey's lines grew north with the progression of time, leading to a mark at eye level and labeled "Feb. 12, 2008."

Then I noticed Claire's first mark, dated May 27, 2000, when she was born. Just below that line we recorded our memory of her twin sibling, who was lost in a miscarriage. With a 409-drenched rag in hand, I tried to erase the lines, but I couldn't seem to do it. It was too messy.

I called my buddy, Troy. "Don't do anything drastic," he said. "I'll be over in two minutes."

When he arrived, he suggested, "I can transplant the marks onto a piece of cardboard or something, if you want."

"No," I said. "That's OK. I don't need the door to tell me how quickly my little girls are growing up."

The door just reminds me that life really is a mist. That is James's point. We can't presume tomorrow; life is a vapor.

3. Follow God's Will

So what are we to do? James goes on to give us his third bit of counsel: Follow God's will.

"You ought to say, 'If it is the Lord's will, we will live and do this or that.' As it is, you boast in your arrogant schemes. All such boasting is evil" (James 4:15, 16).

Don't brag about your future plans. What assurance do you really have that you'll even be drawing breath tomorrow? Instead, seek to carry out God's will—today.

What is the will of God? I appreciate John Ogilvie's answer: "The restless search for the will of God is a sure sign that you are out of it! The will of God is not a mysterious set of sealed orders we search for and receive if we happen to hit on the right formula. Rather, the will of God is a relationship with Him in which He discloses His purpose, power, and plan for our lives—and in that order."[3]

Here is our destiny: God calls us to live in a relationship with Him. As we stay connected to Him, we experience His purpose, power, and plan for our lives.

As you contemplate God's will for your life, it is not about guessing the right school, career, mate and so on. Instead, it's about being faithful in the present. Nurture your relationship with Him today. Rather than asking how you can know His will, seek the answer to this question: "How can I know God—today?" And then, as you live in His presence, He will guide you. His perfect plan, which is your destiny, will then unfold.

4. Do Good

Finally, James reminds us to do the good we know we should do. He writes:

"If anyone, then, knows the good they ought to do and doesn't do it, it is sin for them" (James 4:17).

How's that for some punchy advice on living your destiny? Do good. Live connected to Jesus and you will know the good He has summoned you to perform. So go do it. Today. You will then be well on your way to crafting the lofty legacy God envisions just for you.

Your life is a mist, true enough. It's here today, gone tomorrow. But that's not to say that your mist is meaningless. In this one short shot you have in this world, do good. Impact the place in a way that cannot be ignored.

To show you what this looks like, let's close out the chapter with a few stories I've collected through the years of some ordinary kids who leveraged their mist in extraordinary ways to make some serious waves around the world.

William Dunckelman, a 14-year-old from Houma, Louisiana, claims, "The power to make a positive difference in this world lies within all of us, regardless of age. It is important to find a cause closest to your heart, and let this heartfelt passion be your guide."

He discovered a project close to his heart while visiting a nursing home. It occurred to him that the arts could enhance the lives of senior citizens, so he launched Project FAME (Fine Arts Motivating the Elderly). Thanks to William's efforts, nursing-home residents in 35 states have received more than $155,000 worth of art supplies, books, CDs, and DVDs.

His work didn't stop there. Not only does he spend countless hours with Project FAME—he has also managed to raise and donate more than $26,000 worth of toys, books, and clothing to the impoverished in the Houma community. Marissa Bagala, a local teacher, said of William:

"As an educator, I am often faced with youth searching for a purpose in life. It is with hope that I have witnessed William serve as a role model for children who are seeking purpose. Truly, it is rare to meet such a motivated, caring young person. He allows us to look beyond the challenges our world faces today and recognizes the promise of tomorrow."[4]

Another story that has inspired me is that of Brittany Bergquist. When she was 13, she heard about an American soldier in Iraq who ran up a $7,624 phone bill by calling home. Determined to help, Brittany solicited funds from her 12-year-old brother, Robbie. Together they pooled their $21 and vowed to make a difference. Their dream was a lofty one: to assist all service members in calling home for free. Thus began the organization Cell Phones for Soldiers. Wikipedia.com offers this update on their little project:

"By 2009 . . . the family had raised more than 2 million dollars, which provided members of the U.S. Armed Forces with more than 500,000 one-hour calling cards. That's more than 30 million minutes of connection with family and friends at home."[5]

Another teenager I find inspiring is Laura Greer of Miami, Florida. When she was 17, Laura wrote the book *The Foster Care Guide for Kids*. The idea came while Laura was volunteering at a local shelter for abused children. She found that many of the kids were confused about what was happening to them. "I tried to gently explain their situation," she said, "but I knew my explanations weren't enough."

Laura searched for resources explaining foster care in kids' language, but came up empty—so she wrote her own book. Next, she solicited $35,000 to cover printing and distribution costs. Since then, "Laura's book has been approved by the Florida Department of Children and Families, and distributed to numerous foster-care providers and child welfare organizations. In addition, the Miami Dade County Public School System has distributed copies to school psychologists, social workers, and counselors throughout the district."[6]

One more snapshot of a kid carving out a legacy not to be missed: Iqbal Masih was only 4 years old when sold to a carpet factory owner for 600 rupees—roughly $12. For the next six years he was chained to a carpet-weaving loom and forced to work up to 14 hours a day, seven days a week, tying tiny carpet knots. He was physically and verbally abused, and lack of food stunted his growth.

At age 10, in 1992, Iqbal and other kids defied their owners and attended the Bonded Labor Liberation Front's (BLLF) Freedom Day celebration. He learned that it was illegal to enslave kids, but the law was seldom enforced. Iqbal gave an impromptu speech at that meeting that local newspapers published. Soon afterward, the BLLF helped Iqbal gain his freedom and then provided his schooling. Wanting to become a lawyer, Iqbal said, "My dream is to end child labor for all the children of the world."

At age 12, in 1994, he traveled throughout the United States and Europe as a BLLF spokesperson, calling for an end to child labor and a boycott of

Pakistan's carpet industry. He became world-renowned for his efforts and achievements, and received Reebok's Youth in Action Award.

Iqbal's bravery helped to free many kids, but speaking out cost him his life. On Easter Sunday, April 16, 1995, while he rode a bike near his home, an unknown assailant shot and killed the 12-year-old.

But the story doesn't end there. Students of Broad Meadows Middle School in Quincy, Massachusetts, where Iqbal had spoken, were shocked and outraged. In his memory they launched a fund-raising campaign requesting symbolic $12 donations. They raised more than $150,000 for a Pakistani school, named in his honor, that opened in 1997.

Long after the mist of Iqbal's short life evaporated, his story continues to inspire and motivate. Though he didn't have much time in this world, he changed it just the same.

You, too, have one short life. You have no guarantee for tomorrow. So while God gives you today, make a difference. Follow His will. Do good.

---

[1] www.preachingtoday.com/illustrations/2006/october/1100206.html (accessed Mar. 6, 2012).

[2] Ruth Schenk, "What Changes When You Only Have 24 Hours to Live?" *Southeast Outlook,* July 1, 2010, www.preachingtoday.com/illustrations/2010/august/3082310.html (accessed Mar. 6, 2012).

[3] http://thenetrev.wordpress.com/2012/02/29/are-we-full-of-our-grandiose-selves/ (accessed Mar. 6, 2012).

[4] http://phx.corporate-ir.net/phoenix.zhtml?c=182478&p=irol-newsArticle_print&ID=654555&highlight= (accessed Mar. 6, 2012).

[5] http://en.wikipedia.org/wiki/Cell_Phones_for_Soldiers (accessed Mar. 6, 2012).

[6] http://goliath.ecnext.com/coms2/gi_0199-2466697/Florida-s-Top-Two-Youth.html (accessed Mar. 5, 2012).

Two Cents
of Significance

Fred Craddock, emeritus professor of preaching and New Testament at Emory University, said in an address to ministers, "To give my life for Christ appears glorious. To pour myself out for others . . . to pay the ultimate price of martyrdom—I'll do it. I'm ready, Lord, to go out in a blaze of glory."

That's the kind of glorious bravado you'd expect to find in a book about destiny, calling, and purpose, right? But then Craddock gets personal:

"We think giving our all to the Lord is like taking a $1,000 bill and laying it on the table—'Here's my life, Lord. I'm giving it all.'

"But the reality for most of us is that He sends us to the bank and has us cash in the $1,000 for quarters. We go through life putting out 25 cents here and 50 cents there. Listen to the neighbor kid's troubles instead of saying 'Get lost.' Go to a committee meeting. Give a cup of water to a shaky old man in a nursing home.

"Usually giving our life to Christ isn't glorious. It's done in all those little acts of love, 25 cents at a time. It would be easy to go out in a flash of glory; it's harder to live the Christian life little by little over the long haul."*

That's how your life gets spent—little by little, two cents at a time. And if you're ever tempted to think your two cents don't add up to much, consider the story of the widow who didn't even have two cents.

The Broke Widow

Here's the story: "As Jesus looked up, he saw the rich putting their gifts into the temple treasury. He also saw a poor widow put in two very small copper coins. 'Truly I tell you,' he said, 'this poor widow has put in more than all the others. All these people gave their gifts out of their wealth; but she out of her poverty put in all she had to live on'" (Luke 21:1-4).

Being Passover time, Jerusalem would have swollen to roughly three times its normal population. Most of the visitors were rich; after all, they had resources to use for travel. So Jesus observes the Donald Trumps of the world flashing gold-stuffed wallets and loading up the Temple treasury.

Then a woman from the opposite end of the socioeconomic spectrum slinks onto the stage. The ancient world called widows "the silent ones" since they had no one to care for or speak for them. But notice, she wasn't just a widow. The text labels her a *poor* widow. All widows were poor. This woman, then, was destitute.

She plops two lepta into the plate. A lepton had the least value of any coin. A literal translation renders it "the thin one." In today's currency it would be worth one fortieth of a penny, making her offering a whopping one twentieth of a cent. To say the woman didn't have two cents is not an exaggeration.

What was going on in her head at that moment?

God surely doesn't need my two coins. That guy, he just put a million of these here coins in there. God can sure do something big with that offering, but mine? I'm pitiful. But I got nuttin' else. No savings. No food. No cow. The only thing I got, I ain't even got anymore—I just gave it to God. It's not like God needs my sorry little sacrifice.

Or perhaps her thoughts tracked something like this:

God is so good. He has given me everything. He has always provided for me—when I was a little girl, then when I was a young woman and got married, and then when the love of my life died—every day God has been so faithful. When nobody else had time to listen to me, God was there. My offering ain't much, but it's all I got. And I'm glad to give it all to my God.

Maybe she thought about the Passover—ruminating about the sacrificial lamb and God's sacrificial love. Perhaps she envisioned Him providing bread to His children every day for 40 years. Or she might have considered His faithfulness in leading His people into the Promised Land.

One thing she knew was that nobody would notice her gift. Others dropped heavy silver and gold coins that clanked loudly. That clanging broadcast their "righteousness."

But the clink of her two very small copper coins? Nobody would notice.

Ah, but Someone did. She didn't see the Rabbi who got all choked up at her gift. The woman didn't know that this Rabbi's mom was also a widow. And she didn't hear Him say that her gift was more than all the others.

Nor could she have known that He was agonizing over a sacrifice that

He would make during that same Passover. It was the week of His death. As He watched her, perhaps He prayed, "Abba, if she can trust You like that, so can I. If she can give everything to You, I will go to the cross and give everything too."

Surely she did not know that millennia would pass, empires would rise and fall, corporations would ascend and then be forgotten, but the sound of her two coins would echo throughout time. She had no idea just how substantial her offering was.

Your Two Cents' Worth

The point is, you too may think your two cents aren't worth much. But you would be wrong. Your life, invested two measly cents at a time, can have an impact for eternity.

Just crunch the numbers. It is estimated that if the widow's mite had been deposited at the "First National Bank, Jerusalem" to draw 4 percent interest semiannually, the fund today would total more than $4,800,000,000,000,000,000,000! It's hard to label that as insignificant, huh?

Let's take that number ($4.8 sextillion) and call it your life. Sure, it sounds super spiritual to present the whole caboodle to God, but that's not how it works. Your sacrifice, your life—your destiny, if you will—gets split up into trillions of tiny offerings. During the course of your life, those insignificant gifts add up. Before you know it, your contribution is quite weighty indeed.

You see, God put you in this world to throw your two cents into the mix today, then again tomorrow, and the next day, and so on. Soon your coins help to create a beautiful mosaic of a changed and better world in which God's redemptive narrative plays out through your life. That's why you are here.

Your gifts to God, of course, are not just pennies you plunk into the plate. Don't think that money is the only way to make a contribution. Kingdom investment opportunities are everywhere. Train your eye and tune your heart, and you'll discover a zillion ways to make deposits into God's bank.

So why not invest your two cents? Give blood. Volunteer at the animal shelter. Send an anonymous gift to someone in need. Deliver daisies to the hospital. Babysit for a single parent. Adopt a stray cat. Push a wheelchair. Rake a widow's lawn. Fill up your unemployed friend's car with gas. Play your violin at the local hospice. Get out of the pew and into the world, where kingdom opportunities are as plentiful as pennies.

Those tiny offerings of grace may not seem like much, but given enough time, with enough people, we can create a symphony of grace that will rock the world.

Look around, and you'll see lots of "widows" stepping up to the plate.

Johnny the Bagger

Take, for example, Johnny the Bagger, 19 years old. He works in a grocery store. After attending a training event for cashiers and stockers, Johnny wanted to give his two cents. The conference speaker, Barbara Glanz, urged everyone to seize opportunities to be a blessing, to invest their two cents in making the world a better place. When the session ended, she left her number and invited anyone to call her if they wanted to talk further about something she had said.

About a month later Barbara received a call from Johnny. After proudly informing her that he had Down syndrome, he said, "Barbara, I liked what you talked about. But I didn't think I could do anything special for our customers. After all, I'm just a bagger."

Then he had an idea: He decided that every night when he came home from work, he would find a "thought for the day" for his next shift. It would be something positive, some reminder of how good it was to be alive, or how much people mattered, or how many blessings we all enjoy for which we ought to be thankful. If he couldn't find one, he would make something up.

Every night his dad would help him enter the sayings six times on a page on the computer. Printing 50 pages, he would cut out 300 copies and sign each one. Each time Johnny finished bagging someone's groceries, he would slip his saying into the last bag. Then he would stop what he was doing, look the person straight in the eye, and say, "I've put a great saying in your bag. I hope it helps you have a good day. Thanks for coming here."

A month later the store manager phoned Barbara and said, "You won't believe what's happened here. I was making my rounds, and when I got to the cashiers, the line at Johnny's checkout was three times longer than anyone else's. It went all the way down the frozen food aisle."

The manager told her that he had announced that other checkout lines were open, but none of the customers volunteered to move. They said, "That's OK. We'll wait. We want to be in Johnny's line." One woman came up to him, grabbed his arm, and said, "I used to shop in your store once a week. Now I come in every time I go by—I want to get Johnny's thought for the day."

Johnny was doing more then bagging groceries—he was filling lives with hope. He was using his life to invest his two cents' worth and, consequently, he was enriching the lives of many in some very significant ways.

A few months later the manager called Barbara once again to tell her how Johnny was transforming the whole store. He reported that when the floral department had a broken flower or unused corsage, they used to throw it away. Now they go out in the aisles, find an elderly woman or a little girl, and pin it on her. The butchers started putting ribbons on the cuts of meat they wrapped up for the customers. Even the guy that repairs shopping carts was trying to make sure that all the carts had wheels that actually worked.

And all the shoppers from every nation and kindred and tribe and tongue and people will be blessed through Johnny—a lowly bagger whose two cents accounted for a monumental investment in building the kingdom of God.

Mr. B. Virdot

In December 1933 a strange ad appeared in the Canton, Ohio, newspaper: "Man Who Felt Depression's Sting to Help 75 Unfortunate Families." It came from a source that nobody in town could identify—a certain "Mr. B. Virdot." The announcement instructed potential recipients to write a letter describing their need and mail it to General Delivery.

Given the bankrupt economy at the time, requests poured in.

"They turned off our heat . . ."

"Our kids are hungry . . ."

"My husband lost his job . . ."

Every citizen in Canton was aware of Mr. Virdot's offer. But of the 105,000 residents, nobody knew Mr. Virdot. Who was this man? Was it a twisted joke? Might there be an actual payout for people crazy enough to hope?

Sure enough! Checks arrived in the mail, every one signed "B. Virdot."

For decades the mystery went unsolved. Then in 2008 a grandson discovered a dusty briefcase stored away in his parents' attic. Stacked inside were the letters and 150 canceled checks. Mr. B. Virdot was Samuel J. Stone.

His pseudonym combined the names of his three daughters, Barbara, Virginia, and Dorothy.

Samuel J. Stone came from a Pittsburgh ghetto. He had little education. His father was abusive, forcing Samuel and his six siblings to roll cigars in their attic instead of going to school.

Soon Samuel left home to find employment on a barge, then later in a coal mine. By the time of the Depression, he enjoyed a modest income as the owner of a few clothing stores. He was never particularly rich, but the two cents he invested with his life remain an inspiration nearly a century later.

Jenni Ware and Carolee Hazard

On August 11, 2009, Jenni Ware found herself stranded at the Trader Joe's in Menlo Park, California. Her wallet was gone. Her already-hectic day had gotten a lot worse. That's when Carolee Hazard, a complete stranger, approached the distressed Ware and offered to pay the $207 bill. Ware gratefully accepted and promised to repay her. Once home, Hazard posted on Facebook what had transpired, adding that she was "vacillating between feeling really good and very, very stupid." Friends reassured her that she had done the right thing.

The next day Hazard received a thank-you card and a check for $300 in the mail. In the note, Ware suggested that Hazard use the extra $93 to get a massage. But Hazard didn't want a massage; she wanted to do something else with the money. However, she couldn't decide what that might be. So she posted the problem to her Facebook friends, asking what she should do with the extra cash. One of her friends suggested she give the money to the Second Harvest Food Bank of Silicon Valley, an organization whose mission is "to help feed hungry people by picking up and preparing excess fresh food and delivering it daily to social service agencies in Toronto." Hazard liked the idea, so she matched the $93 with her own money and sent in a check to the Second Harvest Bank for $186.

But the giving didn't stop there. As more and more people heard the story, they wanted to join the spontaneously formed "93 Dollar Club." A week later Hazard and Ware reconnected and learned that the massage money had blossomed into $2,000 through the spontaneous generosity of Facebook friends. Ware then posted the story to *her* Facebook page, and the giving continued. Children donated 93 cents of their allowance. One single mom, working 20 hours a week while in grad school, offered $9.30

because she couldn't afford $93. Then the media picked up the story, and more donations poured in. Many chose to give $93 to their own local food banks around the country.

What started out as a simple investment of kindness has led to contributions of more than $120,000 to benefit the Second Harvest Food Banks of San Mateo and Santa Clara counties. Every dollar means two meals, so the money raised thus far accounts for 240,000 meals. With help from posting and reposting on Facebook, the story continues to inspire people to fight hunger—not only in Silicon Valley but around the world.

So now it's your turn. Send in your two cents or 93 cents or $93, or whatever you've got. Put it all out there to make a difference. Just don't underestimate the value of your contribution. Your two cents can have eternal significance.

---

* www.findthepower.net/CP/IL/PostNewABC2_I.php?IL=ON&SeeAlso=HERE%20 I%20AM (accessed Mar. 5, 2012).

I Will Never Happen Again

My friend Pastor Mark Witas tells a delightful story of a troubled fourth grader whom we'll call Jared. While this kid's misdeeds were never Bonnie-and-Clyde bad, they were frequent and malicious enough to score a firm threat from the principal. He said to Jared, "One more misstep—no matter how minor—and we will have to dismiss you from this school."

The next morning Jared's teacher noticed something strange going on. She saw a rainbow of colored stripes streaking down from Jared's nose. One more time Jared was off to that familiar place in the principal's office.

"You give me no choice," the official explained, "I clearly told you that this time we'd insist that you not come back to school."

"But please," Jared begged, "some kid put Skittles on my desk, and I knew I'd be in big trouble if the teacher found them there, so I hid them as quickly as I could. The only place to hide them was in my nose."

The principal's stern face softened, and then he conceded, "OK, if you write a paper to the disciplinary committee to promise that this will indeed be the last problem we have with you, then maybe, just maybe, they will make an exception."

Jared wrote the paper that night. He meant to start it by saying "*It* will never happen again." A minor typo, however, rendered the statement as "*I* will never happen again."

He made a mistake. Or did he? Perhaps his typo is truer than his intended thought.

"*I* will never happen again." Yes, I only have one shot at life—one chance to get it right on this earth. Sure, my life may be only one of billions of other lives, and perhaps my life only contributes two cents to the World Bank, but as we learned in the previous chapter, that two cents can be a windfall for humanity.

I am here on this earth to leverage a couple small coins that can contribute to the world in a big way. So how do I do this? How can I use my life for maximum impact? How can I make it *really* count?

Perhaps the best person to answer such a question is someone at the sunset of life, a wise individual at the finish line who can enlighten those of us who are a few paces behind.

Let me introduce you to that someone: Paul is a convict awaiting execution on death row. In a few hours he will be dead, so he picks up his quill and journals his final thoughts in a letter to a young preacher named Timothy. From his vantage point, Paul has a unique perspective. He has no time to write about trivial matters. In such moments the purpose of life finds clarity. As you would expect, his letter cuts to the weightiest issues of life and what it means to be human. It drips with wisdom born from decades of experience. Knowing his letter will be his final epitaph, Paul challenges Pastor Timothy to make his life count for something.

Most helpful, he deals with that all-important question of "How?" Everybody wants to live a life that counts. Where we often get tripped up is that we're murky on how to do it. So let's mine the major themes of 2 Timothy and discover the apostle's blueprint for a meaningful life.

Die for a Worthwhile Cause

First, Paul invites Timothy to join him in dying for a worthwhile cause:

"So do not be ashamed of the testimony about our Lord or of me his prisoner. Rather, join with me in suffering for the gospel, by the power of God" (2 Tim. 1:8).

The apostle is gladly cashing in his life on earth for the sake of the gospel. He invites Timothy to do the same. After all, is there a more worthwhile investment of one's life? Paul would emphatically argue, "No!" He unapologetically challenges Timothy to suffer for a worthy cause—the gospel.

The harsh reality is this: You will die. And so will I. Furthermore, you will die for a cause. For some, that cause is nothing more than a higher score on Angry Birds, a lower handicap at the country club, or another trip to the outlet mall.

What is so important to you that you would die for it?

For Myrtle Young, it's potato chips. While employed at Seyfert's Foods, Inc., Myrtle collected chips that look like animals, objects, or in some way reflect the physiognomy or profile of famous people. With a quarter million pounds of potatoes passing in front of her daily, she chip-napped some doozies through the years.

Myrtle became world-famous for her collection. She was featured on *Late Night With David Letterman*, *The Tonight Show*, and a host of other programs that provided a platform for her to talk about her all-consuming passion—potato chips.

In September 1990, 66-year-old Myrtle displayed about 75 chips from her collection at a retirement expo in Fort Wayne, Indiana. She joined other senior citizens who shared their own enthusiasms. For some it was pictures of family members and intricate family trees. For another man it was dachshunds.

"There were quite a few people standing around, and I was telling them about my chip collection," Myrtle recalls. "This one man reached through quickly and took one."

Gregory Hough assumed they were samples. No sooner did he pop the chip replica of a sand dollar into his mouth than a salesperson for Seyfert's collared him and shouted, "Spit it out!" When he did, to Myrtle's horror the potato chip sand dollar was ruined.

Reporters later asked Hough how the chip tasted, and he said, "That thing was stale." After all, it was 2 years old.

Myrtle Wood told news reporters, "I'm so glad he didn't grab Bob Hope. If he had grabbed him, I'd probably be in a hospital."[1]

In the hospital? After losing a potato chip? Really?

Hey, we all gotta die for something.

A conversation comes to mind with a kid who confessed, "Pastor, I never have devotions. I have no devotional life."

I didn't want to quibble over semantics, but I couldn't help myself. I had to correct him. "You do have devotions every day," I countered. "Everybody is devoted to something. Maybe your devotion is focused on school, sports, or your girlfriend, but we all have devotion—to something."

Whatever you are devoted to is what you will die for. So what are you willing to perish for? Money? Success? Family? Potato chips? We all die for some cause. Paul says to choose one worthwhile.

Join in Suffering

In the next chapter of 2 Timothy Paul tells us to "join with [him] in suffering" (2 Tim. 2:3). To highlight his point, Paul offers three metaphors of endurance: "a good soldier" (verse 3); "an athlete" (verse 5); and "the hardworking farmer" (verse 6).

Soldiers, athletes, and farmers all understand the inevitable hardship that plagues any high-impact player on the road to success. Want to make a difference with your life? Don't expect the journey to be easy.

Louis Zamperini was both an athlete and a soldier. And he knows a bit about enduring hardship. His amazing story appears in Laura Hillenbrand's New York *Times* best seller *Unbroken: A World War II Story of Survival, Resilience, and Redemption*.

Zamperini competed in the 5,000-meter race at the 1936 Olympic games in Berlin, Germany. His promising future as an athlete, however, soon gave way to his new career as a second lieutenant in the United States Army Air Force during World War II.

On May 27, 1943, Zamperini's bomber left Oahu in search of survivors from a downed plane. After traveling nearly 800 miles from base, the bomber plunged into the ocean. Zamperini and another soldier would set a world record for survival at sea—47 days of fighting sharks, starvation, dehydration, and dementia.

At last they reached the Marshall Islands, only to be captured by the Japanese Navy. The hardship intensified. Zamperini spent the next two years as a prisoner of war in Japan's Sugamo Prison. Tormented by the sadistic prison guard Mutsuhiro Watanabe (nicknamed "The Bird"), Zamperini endured unrelenting physical torture and verbal humiliation— all done in an attempt to shatter the spirit of the American soldiers.

In 1944, after Zamperini had been declared dead, he returned to America to a rush of publicity. Sadly, his life spiraled into a prison of his own making—one of alcoholism and rage. He suffered constant nightmares about his past and battled an obsessive drive to murder The Bird. But the walls of addiction and hatred crumbled in 1949 when Zamperini attended a Billy Graham crusade and accepted Christ as his personal Savior.

In the words of Laura Hildenbrand: "When [Louie] thought of his history, what resonated with him now was not all that he had suffered but the divine love that he believed had intervened to save him. He was not the worthless, broken, forsaken man that The Bird had striven to make him. In a single, silent moment, his rage, his fear, his humiliation and helplessness, had fallen away. That morning, he believed, he was a new creation."[2]

The impact of Zamperini's life has been remarkable. Now in his 90s and still speaking to thousands of people, he continues to inspire millions.

If you're looking for a poster boy for making your life count, Louis Zamperini should take top consideration. Remember, though, that central to his story is the unsavory bite of hardship. Anybody who leaves a major mark in our world understands that hardship is simply part of the process.

Continue

The third nugget of counsel that Paul offers Timothy is to continue. He writes:

"Continue in what you have learned and have become convinced of" (2 Tim. 3:14).

"Stay the course" is Paul's message. You are convicted that your life is no accident, your calling is a noble one and your mission anointed, so keep plowing ahead. Continue, continue, continue.

God's plan for your life may be more than you dare to imagine. Don't limit the Almighty with your myopic vision. That is why it is so important to stay on the path on which God has placed you. Trust Him to lead you to places that are inaccessible through human ingenuity alone. Don't flake on God's calling just because cynics say your dreams are impossible. "With God, all things are possible" (Matt. 19:26).

George Dantzig comes to mind as someone who discovered that doing the impossible is possible. In 1939, during his first year as a doctoral student at the University of California, Berkeley, Dantzig arrived late for a class taught by Jerzy Neyman, one of the great founders of modern statistics. Dantzig copied down the two problems on the blackboard and took them home to solve. Day after day, night after night, he choked on the challenges. Never had he struggled so over a couple math problems.

Several days later Dantzig, at last, finished the equations. "I'm sorry I'm so late with the homework," he said to Neyman.

"Oh, yeah," the distracted professor replied. "Just leave it on the desk."

Six weeks later, on a Sunday morning, Neyman banged on Dantzig's door. The problems that Dantzig had assumed were homework were actually unproven statistical theorems that Neyman used as examples of problems that simply could not be solved—and Dantzig had proved both of them. Both were eventually published, with Dantzig as coauthor.

"When I began to worry about a thesis topic," Dantzig later recalled, "Neyman just shrugged and told me to wrap the two problems in a binder and he would accept them as my thesis."[3]

When you're tired of trying, when you're fighting the impulse to quit, remember George Dantzig. Stay the course. Maybe you'll be remembered as the person who proved that the impossible is possible.

Preach the Word

The closing appeal that Paul gives to Timothy is this:

"Preach the word; be prepared in season and out of season; correct, rebuke and encourage—with great patience and careful instruction" (2 Tim. 4:2).

In other words, use your life to communicate a message that really matters.

Evangelist Billy Graham attempted to "preach the word" everywhere he went. Whenever he would interact with people at the dry cleaners, gas station, or library, Graham would preach the Word.

For 23 years the A. Larry Ross firm handled Graham's media and public relations. Ross recounts:

"Almost always before a TV interview, they do a microphone check, and they ask the interviewee to say something—anything—so they can adjust the audio settings. Often a corporate executive, for that check, will count to ten, say their ABCs, or recite what he had for breakfast. Mr. Graham would always quote John 3:16—'For God so loved the world that he gave his only begotten Son, that whosoever believeth in him shall not perish but have everlasting life.'

"When I asked Mr. Graham why he does that, he replied, 'Because that way, if I am not able to communicate the gospel clearly during the interview, at least the cameraman will have heard it.'"[4]

Even in the preinterview time, Graham focused on his overriding purpose in life.

What's your purpose in life? Does it bleed through all your activities? Truth is, you can fulfill God's intent for your life. How? Lose yourself in a worthwhile cause. Join in suffering. Continue. And preach the Word.

Whatever you do, don't put it off. Start today. Just remember: You will never happen again.

---

[1] http://news.google.com/newspapers?nid=1755&dat=19900917&id=S_YcAAAAIBAJ&sjid=pXoEAAAAIBAJ&pg=5602,2885110.

[2] Laura Hildenbrand, *Unbroken* (New York: Random House, 2010), p. 376.

[3] www.tumblr.com/tagged/george-dantzig (accessed Mar. 7, 2012).

[4] Harold Myra and Marshall Shelley, *The Leadership Secrets of Billy Graham* (Grand Rapids: Zondervan, 2005), pp. 71, 72.

Dying Rich
Versus Living Rich

Question C. Wright Mills as to why you're here, and he'll tell you it's to make money—a lot of money.

"Of all the possible values of human society, one and one only is the truly sovereign, truly universal, truly sound, truly and completely acceptable goal of man in America. That goal is money, and let there be no sour grapes about it from the losers."[1]

Maybe the old bumper sticker ("He who dies with the most toys wins") has it right. And maybe not. Lots of people die with a wad of money, but their death punctuates a bilious life. They die rich, but they live so poorly.

John Lennon, one of the founding members of the Beatles, died with acres of toys. In 1980 he was shot outside the Dakota building in New York City, leaving an estate valued at $550 million. But what kind of legacy did he pass on? His son, Julian, whom John had abandoned when the boy was 5, answers:

"The only thing my dad taught me was how not to be a father."

Later, in an interview published in the Calgary *Herald*, Julian elaborated:

"From my point of view, I felt he was a hypocrite. Dad could talk about peace and love out loud to the world, but he could never show it to the people who supposedly meant the most to him—his wife and son. How can you talk about peace and love and have a family in bits and pieces—no communication, adultery, divorce? You can't do it, not if you're being true and honest with yourself."[2]

Someone once said to Paul McCartney, "But the Beatles were anti-materialistic. How is it that Lennon left behind such a fortune?"

McCartney replied, "Anti-materialistic? That's a huge myth. John and I literally used to sit down and say, 'Now let's write a swimming pool.'"

Lennon died a rich man. But did he *live* as a rich man? And which is more important?

A Story of an Empty Life Full of Stuff (Luke 12:13-21)

Jesus once told a story similar to John Lennon's. It's the same old tale of a ton of toys at death tacked to the end of a regrettable life. Let's review the story:

"Someone in the crowd said to him, 'Teacher, tell my brother to divide the inheritance with me' " (Luke 12:13).

Although it was a common practice in ancient Palestine for people to take their unsettled disputes to respected rabbis, Jesus refused to get involved in the quarrel.

"Jesus replied, 'Man, who appointed me a judge or an arbiter between you?' Then he said to them, 'Watch out! Be on your guard against all kinds of greed; life does not consist in an abundance of possessions' " (verses 14, 15).

Our Savior makes it clear that the goal of life is not to die rich. The value of your life will not be measured by that of the portfolio you leave behind.

So Jesus told them the following parable: "The ground of a certain rich man yielded an abundant harvest. He thought to himself, 'What shall I do? I have no place to store my crops' " (verses 16, 17).

Notice that Jesus labels him a "rich man" with a productive crop. In other words, the rich get richer. As the story unfolds, however, it is clear that he was a poor rich man. Like the Laodicean church, he was rich, increased with goods, having need of nothing, yet bankrupt in the things that really matter in life.

"Then he said, 'This is what I'll do. I will tear down my barns and build bigger ones, and there I will store my grain. And I'll say to myself, "You have plenty of grain laid up for many years. Take life easy; eat, drink and be merry" ' " (verses 18, 19).

The man had an insatiable appetite for more. He was like Dennis Levine, the partner of Ivan Boesky who traded illegally on Wall Street with insider information. He made a fortune until busted. Levine later reflected:

"People always ask, 'Why would somebody who's making over $1 million a year start trading on inside information?' . . . At the root of my compulsive trading was an inability to set limits. Perhaps it's worth noting that my legitimate success stemmed from the same root. My ambition was so strong it went beyond rationality, and I gradually lost sight of what constitutes ethical behavior. At each new level of success I set higher goals, imprisoning myself in a cycle from which I saw no escape. When I became a senior vice president, I wanted to be a managing director, and when I became a managing director, I wanted to be a client. If I was making $100,000 a year, I thought, *I can make $200,000.* And if I made $1 million, *I can make $3 million.* And so it went."[3]

And so it goes. It's never quite enough, is it? It reminds me of the old joke, "Who is happier—a millionaire or the man with 10 kids?" Answer: "The man with 10 kids, because the millionaire still wants more."

Notice the harsh indictment against the parable's rich man:

"But God said to him, 'You fool! This very night your life will be demanded from you. Then who will get what you have prepared for yourself?'" (verse 20).

Here is extremely harsh language, from God Himself. "You fool!" He said.

One time, when I was a kid, I screamed at my brother Paul, "Shut up, you fool."

Dad overheard me and barked, "Karl, you go to your room this instant. And don't come out until you have found and memorized the verse in the Bible that says anyone who calls his brother a fool will burn in hell."

"But Paul's the one who—"

"I'll deal with Paul. You go find that verse."

I marched to my room like a soldier on strike. Slumping onto my bed, I rehearsed my assignment. *Surely,* I thought, *there's not really a verse that says that if we call our brother a fool we're going to fry in hell. Why would Jesus care what I call Paul?*

Instead of searching through Scripture, I read *Sports Illustrated,* wrote a letter to my grandma, and tinkered with my train set. All the while, however, I wondered if Dad was serious about that verse in the Bible.

An hour later he summoned me. "You find the verse yet?"

"Awwww, Dad," I moaned. "There's not really a verse like that, is there?"

"Absolutely. Now find it. You're not coming out of your room until you do."

"Where should I look?"

"Start in the New Testament—but that's your only hint. Now get on it."

I opened my Bible to the New Testament and quickly scanned the pages of Matthew. And then I saw it. I stared in disbelief.

The verse seemed so harsh. So clear. So condemning. Yet it was there:

"But I say unto you, That whosoever is angry with his brother without a cause shall be in danger of the judgment: and whosoever shall say but to his brother, . . . Thou fool, shall be in danger of hell fire" (Matt. 5:22, KJV).

Feeling as if someone had lashed my soul with barbed wire, I read the verse again. And then again. There seemed no room for misinterpretation.

I have never again called my brother a fool. And yet it is the very word God uses to describe the rich man.

Then Jesus hammers home the punch line:

"This is how it will be with whoever stores up things for themselves but is not rich toward God" (Luke 12:21).

Ouch! One scholar labels this "the most startling parable Jesus ever told." Indeed, after hearing the story, who wants to repeat the mistakes of the fool?

Now, in order to avoid his mistakes, we need to identify them. Let's consider three big ones.

Mistake Number 1: He Never Saw Beyond Himself

Of all the parables Jesus told, this one contains the most personal pronouns. Scan the story and notice all the times you see the words "I," "me," "my," or "mine."

"He thought to himself, 'What shall *I* do? *I* have no place to store *my* crops.'

"Then he said, 'This is what *I'll* do. *I* will tear down *my* barns and build bigger ones, and there *I* will store *my* surplus grain. And *I'll* say to *myself*, "You have plenty of grain laid up for many years. Take life easy; eat, drink and be merry."'"

The man is as self-centered as a hippo is heavy. If you prefer dying rich over living rich, then live like William Barclay's Edith:

"Edith lived in a little world, bounded on the north, south, east, and west by Edith."[4]

Rick Warren hit a raw nerve with his 2002 devotional, *The Purpose-Driven Life*. To date, it has sold more than 52 million copies and has been described as the best-selling nonfiction hardback book in history.[5] He famously begins the book this way:

"It's not about you.

"The purpose of your life is far greater than your own personal fulfillment, your peace of mind, or even your happiness. It's far greater than your family, your career, or even your wildest dreams and ambitions. If you want to know why you were placed on this planet, you must begin with God. You were born *by* his purpose and *for* his purpose.

"The search for the purpose of life has puzzled people for thousands of years. That's because we typically begin at the wrong starting point—ourselves. We ask self-centered questions like What do *I* want to be? What should *I* do with *my* life? What are *my* goals, *my* ambitions, *my* dreams for *my* future? But focusing on ourselves will never reveal our life's purpose. The Bible says, '*It is God who directs the lives of his creatures; everyone's life is in his power.*'

"Contrary to what many popular books, movies, and seminars tell you, you won't discover life's meaning by looking within yourself."[6]

The rich fool tried to find life's meaning by looking within himself, but it didn't work. And it still doesn't.

Mistake Number 2: He Never Saw Beyond His Stuff

The rich fool anchored his identity and purpose in his stuff—his barns, his crops, his grains, and his goods. Have you ever known someone like that? Some friends of ours come to mind. One time one of them called me with an announcement.

"We closed on the house!" she exclaimed. "You and Cherié simply *have* to come by and see it. You won't believe this place!"

"Super," I said, trying to muster at least a tithe of her giddiness. "We can come by tonight."

"Fantastic! But, ah, um, one thing . . ." she stammered. I knew what was coming. Sure enough, she said, "Um, it wouldn't like be a problem for you to get a babysitter for Lindsey when you come over, would it? I mean, we have so many things that a 2-year-old could break, and you know, um, we wouldn't want you to feel bad about—"

"Don't worry," I said. "We won't bring Lindsey. We wouldn't want her to ruin any of your invaluable possessions. I know how important your stuff is to you and Stan."

"Thanks for understanding," she said, clearly missing my sarcasm.

That evening we got the grand tour. It was quite a place. As we strolled through the home, a cleaning woman followed us with a rake to fix the carpet threads so as to erase any footprints. Apparently, if the threads are not all facing the same direction, it's bad carpet karma. After I opened the door into their master bedroom, my friend massaged the handle with her rag and kindly requested I leave any activities that involved direct contact with their stuff to her, you know, since she had the rag and all.

I can't say they are the most recharging friends I know.

Actress Candice Bergen once told about her mother, who also tended to be a little obsessed with her stuff. Bergen remembers the evening when she took her vivacious and energetic daughter to her mom's house for supper. Here's her story:

"My mom lives in a spotless pastel house of pale peaches and delicate mauves, immaculate ivory carpets. A challenge for a child.

"My daughter Chloe, then 11, came bounding into the living room clutching a huge glass of cranberry juice. Before we could suggest the white grape juice alternative, she plopped onto the sofa, accidentally tipping the full glass of red liquid onto the brand-new peach silk upholstery. For a second we all froze. My mother had not yet come into the room, and although her love for Chloe is boundless, this might have pushed the envelope.

"Then, as one, we sprang into action. Soda water, damp sponge, paper towels. Frantic mopping and blotting. Futile blowing. The sound of approaching footsteps. And Chloe adroitly flipped the large cushion over, sinking quickly into it, and announced, grinning, to no one in particular, the words 'Life is good!' "[7]

Got any silk sofas in your life? Do you hang on to your possessions a little too tightly? Maybe God is calling you to grow beyond your stuff by making a sacrifice. Try giving some of your money away. Sponsor a child through World Vision. Clean out the closet and give it to Goodwill. Donate that third car to the church.

And there are still other ways you can attack the pull of materialism in our culture: Invite the neighbors over for a meal. Volunteer at the soup kitchen. Offer to house a foreign student for a year. There are many ways you can hang on to your stuff loosely—you may not die rich, but you'll live rich.

OK, one more mistake we see in the rich fool.

Mistake Number 3: He Never Saw Beyond the Present World

The rich fool made all of his plans as if life on this earth is all there is. Consider this conversation between a young and ambitious lad and an older man:

"What are you doing this summer?"

"I'll probably get a job mowing lawns or something."
"What are you doing next fall?"
"I'll go back to school."
"And then what?"
"Someday I'll graduate."
"And then what?"
"I'll get a job."
"And then what?"
"I'll get married."
"And then what?"
"I'll have kids."
"And then what?"
"I'll retire."
"And then what?"
"I'll die."
"And then what?"
Have you asked yourself: "And then what?"
Jesus calls us to invest in things that will last beyond this world.
Shortly after Steve Jobs died, Steve Lohr wrote about him in the New York *Times:*

"Mr. Jobs made a lot of money over the years, for himself and for Apple shareholders. But money never seemed to be his principal motivation. One day in the late 1990s Mr. Jobs and I were walking near his home in Palo Alto. Internet stocks were getting bubbly at the time, and Mr. Jobs spoke of the proliferation of start-ups, with so many young entrepreneurs focused on an 'exit strategy,' selling their companies for a quick and hefty profit.

" 'It's such a small ambition and sad, really,' Mr. Jobs said. 'They should want to build something, something that lasts.' "[8]

Do you dream of leveraging your life toward something that lasts beyond the present world? Jesus urged us to think long-term when He said something to the effect of "Do not store up for yourselves shiny iPads, razor-thin Airbooks, and slick iPhones—it's such a small ambition and sad, really—because these things will be obsolete next year, and thieves are always keen to steal them. But store up for yourselves treasures in heaven, where technology never needs updating and thieves have been transformed into honest, nonstealing folk" (Matt. 6:19, 20, KHV [Karl Haffner Version]).

Christ's counsel has great wisdom in it. Yep, my money's on the long-term work of God. I want to participate in building something that lasts—namely, a community of followers of Jesus who live, give, and love like Him. The only "exit strategy" I'm conniving is the ultimate departure from earth when Jesus comes to take us home.

I want to live rich—for eternity.

In his book *When the Game Is Over, It All Goes Back in the Box* John Ortberg makes the helpful distinction between being rich and having riches. He contrasts the lives of two men.

The first man was Larry Clarke. When Larry was in his 30s, he quit his job so he could volunteer full-time at his church. He never married, never owned a home, never took extravagant vacations. Since he loved people, his home was open to everyone.

Early one morning Larry was jogging in downtown Milwaukee when a bus struck and killed him. His death devastated his friends and family.

A wake was held for Larry that week. Unsure of the number of attendees, it was scheduled in the chapel. Organizers speculated that the crowd would be a manageable size. After all, Larry had never married, had no children, and no regular job.

People crammed into the chapel. The wake lasted three hours. The line to walk past the casket stretched out the door for blocks. More than 800 mourners stood in line for three hours to honor Larry.

At the memorial service the next day, so many people crammed in the 500-seat chapel that it had to move to the main auditorium. One person after another spoke of how Larry had touched their life. None of those stories recounted Larry's possessions or achievements—all of them remembered his capacity to love. He always put the needs of others above his own. One person at the funeral mentioned how they had once heard Larry say how you'd be surprised at the amount of good food you could find foraging behind Ralph's supermarket. Food gets thrown out, even though it is still packaged and fresh.

That same decade saw the funeral of a man named Armand Hammer. At 92 he was still the chairman of the Occidental Petroleum Company. A billionaire industrialist and philanthropist, he was called a "giant of capitalism and confidante of world leaders" by *USA Today*. After his death, Harvard-educated political scientist Edward Epstein published the dark side of the man's story.

Hammer got his start by laundering money for the Soviet government. Then he obtained more money through a string of broken marriages. His father went to prison for a botched abortion that Armand himself had performed. Neglecting his only son, Armand also hid himself from an illegitimate daughter. He had no friends at Occidental, where he fired his top executives at his whim. When his brother Victor died, Hammer filed a claim of $667,000 against the $700,000 estate, rather than disbursing it to Victor's children and nursing-home-bound wife.

Only a few people attended Hammer's funeral. Conspicuously missing: his son Julian, the members of his two brothers' families, and most of his colleagues at Occidental. In fact, within days of his death, Occidental distanced itself from him (the Web site doesn't even mention him in its history). The pallbearers included his chauffeur, his male nurse, and a couple other personal employees.

"One man was famous, courted, wealthy, connected, powerful, envied, and feared. The other man secretly scrounged for food behind a grocery store and was loved."[9]

One man died rich. The other lived rich. Which one got it right?

---

[1] www.time.com/time/magazine/article/0,9171,949963,00.html (accessed Mar. 7, 2012).

[2] Phil Calloway, *Who Put My Life on Fast-Forward?* (Eugene, Oreg.: Harvest House Publishers, 2002), p. 225.

[3] Dennis B. Levine, "The Inside Story of an Inside Trader," *Fortune*, May 21, 1990, in http://money.cnn.com/magazines/fortune/fortune_archive/1990/05/21/73553/index.htm.

[4] William Barclay, *The Gospel of Luke* (Philadelphia: Westminster Press, 1956), p. 168.

[5] www.christianpost.com/news/rick-warren-embarks-on-follow-up-to-purpose-driven-life-39893/ (accessed Mar. 8, 2012).

[6] Rick Warren, *The Purpose Driven Life* (Grand Rapids: Zondervan, 2002), pp. 17, 18.

[7] Candice Bergen, *The Right Words at the Right Time*, ed. Marlo Thomas (New York: Atria Books, 2002), pp. 18-20.

[8] Steve Lohr, in New York *Times*, Oct. 8, 2011, www.nytimes.com/2011/10/09/business/steve-jobs-and-the-power-of-taking-the-big-chance.html?pagewanted=all (accessed Mar. 7, 2012).

[9] John Ortberg, *When the Game Is Over, It All Goes Back in the Box* (Grand Rapids: Zondervan, 2007), pp. 93-95.

On Purpose

A friend of mine was in a life-threatening auto accident that left him teetering on the edge of death. For months machines coaxed life into his comatose body. When he finally and miraculously awakened to the world, he was clueless about who he was, where he was, or why he was in the hospital. With a lot of time and therapy, he has been able to reassemble some of the fragments from his life before the crash. But he is not the same person I used to know.

A. W. Tozer suggests that all of us are victims of a spiritual coma. When Adam and Eve crashed in the garden, we lost our sense of purpose. Our identity became shrouded, our self-esteem compromised. Having forgotten the reason we exist, we have been confused about who we are, why we are here, and where we are going.

Tozer explains: "This is the condition of the world today, everywhere and in every culture. From the universities to the coal mines, people do not know why they are here. People have a strange moral and spiritual amnesia and do not know their purpose in life, why they were created, or what they are sent to do. Consequently, lives are filled with confusion, reaching out for any explanation. . . . In spite of this confusion, we try to get around somehow. We travel, play golf, drive cars, eat, sleep, look at beautiful things; but they are all shortsighted aspects of our life.

"The enemy of man's soul has successfully sabotaged this search for moral and spiritual identity. He does everything within his extensive power to prevent us from discovering who and what we are."[1]

So we search. In our quest to find purpose in life, we go everywhere. Solomon, also called "The Quester" (see Eccl. 1:1, Message), visited many places in his futile attempts to answer the question "What is the purpose of my life?"

Searching In School

The Quester went to school for some answers. Turns out he did pretty well in the heady world of academia. He pulled straight A's and scored the title "The wisest man who ever lived." He wrote in his journal, "I applied my mind to study and to explore by wisdom all that is done under the heavens" (verse 13).

When Solomon tells us that he "applied [his] mind" to the pursuit of wisdom, he wasn't kidding. First Kings 4:29-31 describes it like this:

"God gave Solomon wisdom and very great insight, and a breadth of understanding as measureless as the sand on the seashore. Solomon's wisdom was greater than the wisdom of all the people of the East, and greater than all the wisdom of Egypt. He was wiser than anyone else, including Ethan the Ezrahite—wiser than Heman, Kalkol and Darda, the sons of Mahol."

Do you know how wise those men were? I don't either, but they were renowned in that day for their brains, and yet compared to Solomon they were intellectual midgets.

Solomon was so smart that when a head of state paid him a visit and grilled him with hard questions, the Bible records that "the queen of Sheba experienced for herself Solomon's wisdom . . . it took her breath away" (1 Kings 10:4, 5, Message).

Not bad. Surely if one could find purpose in knowledge, then the Quester could have ended his search there at Harvard—but he kept on looking.

As Tozer puts it: "Education alone is not the reason we were born. Our purpose is not for the perfecting of our intellectual nature, the education or development of our mind. I am not against education, because the alternative is simple ignorance. Education, however, does not answer the eternal purpose of why I am here."[2]

Searching at Work

So the Quester heads to the office and figures, *If I'm successful at work, then my search for purpose will be over.* So he throws himself into the pursuit of success. "I undertook great projects" (Eccl. 2:4), he writes. Consider these "great projects" that Solomon launched:

"I built houses for myself and planted vineyards. I made gardens and parks and planted all kinds of fruit trees in them. I made reservoirs to water groves of flourishing trees. I bought male and female slaves and had other slaves who were born in my house. I also owned more herds and flocks than anyone in Jerusalem before me. I amassed silver and gold for myself, and the treasure of kings and provinces" (verses 4-8).

Solomon worked hard and flaunted his success. As king of Israel he extended his country's borders farther than any king before or after him. He transformed Israel into a shipping empire. He seized and nationalized the two major trade routes of his day. He was a perennial fixture atop Forbes' List of the World's Wealthiest. First Kings 10:14 tells us that the "weight of gold that Solomon received yearly was 666 talents," or today's equivalent of 25 tons. Imagine that! Every year, in addition to taxes and profits from trades, Solomon received 25 tons of gold. First Kings 10:23, 24 adds that Solomon was "greater in riches and wisdom than all the other kings of the earth. The whole world sought audience with Solomon."

If purpose in life could be found in success at work, then Solomon's search would have been over. But again he was disappointed, and his quest continued.

Searching Through Pleasure

Solomon writes, "I said to myself, 'Come now, I will test you with pleasure to find out what is good.' But that also proved to be meaningless" (Eccl. 2:1).

The Quester pursues pleasure, but discovers only emptiness there as well. Listen to where he looked for pleasure:

"I tried cheering myself with wine" (verse 3).

Then he thinks that perhaps sexual pleasure is the goal of life. Scripture records that he had 1,000 wives and concubines. (This is the smartest guy in the world? And he answered to 1,000 women? Go figure.)

The Quester then proclaims, "I denied myself nothing my eyes desired; I refused my heart no pleasure" (verse 10).

He's like the Cookie Monster, who says, "See cookie. Want cookie. Eat cookie."

That's the Quester: I see it. I want it. I'll get it.

But it wasn't enough.

The Search Is Over

Toward the end of the Quester's journal we discover the only true solution to a life devoid of meaning and purpose. Solomon writes: "Remember your Creator" (Eccl. 12:1).

A. W. Tozer also asserts that remembering our Creator is our only solution in a search for purpose. He writes:

"In the beginning, God created Adam and Eve, placing them in the beautiful garden east of Eden. We have only a little glimpse into the beauty of that mysterious and wondrous world. All we know is that God created it and afterwards said, 'It is good,' meaning that all creation was in absolute harmony with God and fulfilling its ordained purpose."[3]

Solomon then offers this summary: "Now all has been heard; here is the conclusion of the matter: Fear God and keep his commandments, for this is the duty of all mankind" (verse 13).

Herein is the reason we were created: We are called to fear God and keep His commandments. Simply put, our purpose is to bring Him glory. God says: "Everyone who is called by My name, whom I have created for My glory; I have formed him, yes, I have made him" (Isa. 43:7, NKJV).

John Piper explains, "Life is wasted when we do not live for the glory of God. And I mean *all* of life. It is all for His glory."[4]

Everything we do is to glorify God. Paul confirms this:

"So whether you eat or drink or whatever you do, do it all for the glory of God" (1 Cor. 10:31).

So what does it mean in real life to glorify God in everything? In 1946 S. Truett Cathy decided to find out. He founded a company intent on honoring God in everything. It has always been a unique business model to be sure, but the purpose statement is clear:

"To glorify God by being a faithful steward of all that is entrusted to us. To have a positive influence on all who come in contact with Chick-fil-A."

From its humble beginning the company has grown to more than 1,540 Chick-fil-A restaurants across the United States, with more than $4 billion in annual sales in 2011. Cathy's desire to glorify God in everything has framed his understanding of divine purpose. The result has been focused clarity on the reason for both his company and his life.

"Religion is at the key of the family-operated business," says Cathy, whose son Dan is the chief operating officer and whose other son, Bubba, is a vice president. According to the family patriarch, "our decision to close on Sundays was our way of honoring God and directing our attention to things more important than our business." Cathy testified to *Forbes* magazine that "the Lord has never spoken to me, but I feel Chick-fil-A has been His gift."[5]

So how does it all translate in practical terms? Well, the policy of closing all restaurants on Sundays has cost Cathy billions of dollars in business, but he insists that it's worth it because it gives employees a day to spend with God and family. Moreover, Chick-fil-A sponsors a boys and girls camp through a foundation that Cathy established more than 20 years ago. The WinShape Centre Foundation has also sponsored and built 14 foster homes. The WinShape Family Centre offers marital conferences and retreats for entire families. Chick-fil-A has placed a Bible in every school throughout the entire state of Georgia. These are but a few of the many ways that Cathy glorifies God and fulfills His purpose.

Parenthetically, can you imagine what God wants to do with those who keep the true day of worship, the seventh-day Sabbath found in Exodus 20:8-11? If resting on Sundays is nonnegotiable for Truett Cathy and his buisness enterprises, what's the true, biblical Sabbath worth to you? But I disgress. Back to the main point of this illustration.

You, too, were created to honor God and carry out His intent. He did not set you on earth only to excel in school, succeed at work, or experience pleasure. All such pursuits will lead to a dead end apart from God. Instead, your ultimate purpose is to glorify God and to enjoy a friendship with Him.

Elliot Huck, a 14-year-old from Bloomington, Indiana, understands that his ultimate purpose is to glorify God. This is why he decided to skip the National Spelling Bee. Though he had placed forty-fifth out of more than 250 spellers in last year's competition and was expected to do well again, he felt convicted to stay home this time around. More precisely, he felt convicted to stay in *church*. Because the competition took place on his day of worship, he would not compromise his understanding of the biblical commandment to rest on the Sabbath.

"I always try to glorify God with what I do in the spelling bee because He is the one who gave me the talent for spelling," Elliot said. "Now I think I'm going to not spell and try to give glory to God in that. I have just accepted that God knows what's best, and I'm just going to do what He says."[6]

"And this is my prayer: that your love may abound more and more in knowledge and depth of insight, so that you may be able to discern what is best and may be pure and blameless for the day of Christ, filled with the fruit of righteousness that comes through Jesus Christ—to the glory and praise of God" (Phil. 1:9-11). Amen.

---

[1] A. W. Tozer, *The Purpose of Man* (Ventura, Calif.: Regal, 2009), p. 27.
[2] *Ibid.*, p. 40.
[3] *Ibid.*, p. 21.

[4] John Piper, *Don't Waste Your Life* (Wheaton, Ill.: Crossway Books, 2009), p. 32.

[5] Danielle Sonnenberg, "Religious CEOs: Chick-fil-A Founder, S. Truett Cathy," www.minyanville.com/special-features/articles/religious-ceos-s-truett-cathy-chickfila/5/19/2010/id/28281 (accessed Mar. 8, 2012).

[6] Robert King, "Sunday Contest Spells the End for Student," Indianapolis *Star*, Feb. 22, 2007.

"How Can I Know God's Will?" and Other Confusing Questions

So if your primary reason for being on earth is to glorify God, then what does that mean in practical terms? How specific is God's intent for your actual life? Does He care what you eat? wear? drive? How can you know His plan? Does it include a certain school that you're supposed to attend? the right spouse you should marry? the correct career you need to pursue? And what role, if any, does faith play in all of this? Is the church just an antiquated ritual that is at best a sham or at worst a roadblock to authentic spirituality? Let's tackle some of these sticky questions, shall we?

How Specific Is God's Plan for My Life?

One of my favorite people to follow on Twitter is Donald Miller. I'm also a fan of his Web site, as he always has interesting blogs. For example, in one of his posts he suggests that the chances of God having a specific plan for someone's life is 1 in 227.

I was intrigued. Where did he get that number? He explains that for every one person in the Bible for whom God handed down a specific plan, 226 didn't get a precise recipe for life. So according to Miller's calculations, Joseph was the one while his 11 brothers fell into the 226. Go figure. While his argument is tongue-in-cheek, Miller's point is this: We often sit around waiting for God to disclose His exact plan in our lives, but in most cases God seems pretty silent. Miller explains:

"I don't believe God has mapped out a plan for your every day, or even for your every year. My friends who disagree and think God has a specific plan for everybody are mostly sitting around waiting to hear from God. Meanwhile, God's plan for them, apparently, is to shop at Bed Bath and Beyond and quote the latest *Saturday Night Live* skit. Quite the plan."[1]

In my mind a helpful metaphor is a GPS unit. I punch in my desired location, and a woman with an English accent tells me where to go. There have been times she told me to turn right but I went left instead. ("There is a way that appears to be right, but in the end it leads to death" [Prov. 14:12].) Now, she didn't say, "You idiot. I knew your way was going to land you in the lake. I quit! If you're not going to follow my directions, then get your wife to do this stupid job." Instead, she announces, "Recalculating. When safe to do so, execute a U-turn." In other words, she provides guidance toward the ultimate destination. But if I take a wrong turn, she simply recalculates. I have free will to make my own choices.

God has given you free will to decide. He may have a preferred route that leads toward the desired destination, but He's not flummoxed by your detours. Also keep in mind that the ultimate destination is not a specific profession, partner, or plan. It is a Person. To know and glorify Jesus Christ—that is God's plan for your life. The Bible says:

"Now this is eternal life: that they know you, the only true God, and Jesus Christ, whom you have sent" (John 17:3).

So when you make poor choices, God responds by giving you an opportunity to learn from your missteps and then get back on track in your journey toward Jesus. To suggest otherwise is to paint God as a control freak—a notion simply incongruent with His character. What kind of father would spank his child every time the kid pokes a toe beyond a line that marks some explicit plan? Talk about a dysfunctional family! Such an idea undermines the free will that God entrusts to His children. He does not want robots that He can program for every specific action in life. He desires a relationship, not a computer that executes some program He wrote.

Miller compares our lives to an art project in which God provides us with butcher paper and crayons and tells us to draw something beautiful. As our Father and Friend, God gives us guidelines as to what is good, right, pure, and worthy to draw. He also plants within every one of us a heart filled with desire and longing.

Then Miller concludes by suggesting that if God is setting a box of crayons (i.e., your life) in front of you, you need to get drawing!

"[God has] taught you right from wrong, good from bad, beautiful from profane, so draw. He will be with you, proud of you, cheering you on, so draw. He loves you, so draw in the inspiration of the knowledge of His love. Draw a purple horse, a red ocean, a nine-legged dog, it doesn't matter.

Let's stop being so afraid. Let's live, and show the world what it really means to be grateful we don't live in a dysfunctional family."[2]

How Can I Know God's Plan?

Having served as a pastor on a university campus since 1997, I can tell you it's the most common question I've heard through the years. It's always the most requested subject when surveying students about topics they want to hear addressed in sermons. When students make an appointment to see me, I assume that the question they will have for me is "How can I know God's will in my life?"

Of course, the question has come in different shades, but underlying the specifics has been the desire to understand and follow God's plan.

Some years ago I was presenting a guest lecture in a homiletics class when a student hit me with that same old question. "Pastor," he said, "how can I know what God wants me to do after graduation?"

"What do you mean?" I asked.

"Well, sorry to get off the topic of your lecture, but four years ago I sacrificed everything to come to Walla Walla University. At the time a man told me that God had revealed to him in a dream that I was to come be his business manager. I asked him why God didn't mention that I had already sent in my deposit to college. But now that I'm ready to graduate, I have no clue what I'm going to do. I don't know if I can work for the denomination or what. What do you think?"

"Well, um . . . ah . . ." I stammered for time to collect my thoughts.

He picked up his story. "I enrolled in college later in life. I thought it was God's calling to ministry, but now I don't know if it was a big mistake or not. I don't know where I'm going to work."

Setting aside my lecture notes, I said, "I don't know what to say, other than to tell you my own experience. I took a double major in college because I wasn't sure that working for the denomination would really pan out. Then I earned two master's degrees—one in business and one in theology. Again, I wanted to be sure I had options. I never dreamed that all these years later I would still be a pastor of a local church—but here I am, and I love it."

"But maybe my story won't work out like that," he replied.

"It may not," I agreed, "but I wonder if sometimes we ask the wrong question. I know you've probably heard it before, but I always tell students that rather than asking 'How can I know God's will?' I think we should ask 'How can I know God?'"

"What do you mean?"

"Well, when I was trying to decide whether or not to accept a request to pastor in another church, people often asked, 'Do you think God is calling you there?' Frankly, I had a strong sense that God was reassuring me that no matter what decision I made, He would bless me. If I drop out of full-time ministry and become a lawyer or a real estate agent, no doubt I can still please God in those vocations. No matter what my job description, if I continually ask, 'How can I know God?' and then pursue that passion, I can live in the center of His will."

"That's very helpful to hear," the student commented.

"No matter where you're at next year," I said, "God will guide you to the work He has for you, and He will equip you to do it. No matter who signs your checks, God is wanting you to respond to a higher calling than the world can offer you—whether you're a preacher or a printing press operator. Whatever you end up doing, glorify God in it."

At the closing bell I shared a text that I have found personally helpful in answering the student's question:

"Therefore, I urge you, brothers and sisters, in view of God's mercy, to offer your bodies as a living sacrifice, holy and pleasing to God—this is your true and proper worship. Do not conform to the pattern of this world, but be transformed by the renewing of your mind. Then you will be able to test and approve what God's will is—his good, pleasing and perfect will" (Rom. 12:1, 2).

So long as we live in Jesus, connected to Him, we need not fret about the future. We won't need to pull a Nancy Reagan. She is probably best remembered for the scandal in 1987 when former Reagan staffer Donald Regan revealed that she had frequently sought advice from an astrologer, and sometimes changed the president's schedule accordingly. Many Americans were outraged to hear that the president would be so closely aligned with such dubious practices. After all, aren't there better ways to seek guidance?

I certainly think so! One alternative to horoscopes, psychic hotlines, and astrologers is to seek guidance from God. But how does that translate into your life today?

Well, finding guidance from God amid the daily grind of life boils down to living moment by moment, in Christ. Ellen White counsels, "Let God work, and let the human agent walk softly before Him, watching, waiting, praying, looking unto Jesus every moment, led and controlled by the precious Spirit, which is light and life."[3]

So try this: surrender *every* decision today—big and small—to Christ. Live in Jesus every moment. As you eat breakfast, remember that your body is the temple of God. Rather than wolfing down a doughnut on the way out the door, sit down and talk to Jesus.

In your car, picture Jesus in the passenger seat. (If He looks a little nervous, you'll want to slow down or stop your texting!) Being aware that Jesus is right there with you informs how you'll want to react to the rude driver that cut you off.

At school you begin to see people as Jesus views them. You recognize the fat kid who hangs out of his or her T-shirt in PE as a tender, valuable human being rather than a geek to ignore. More and more you find yourself responding to people in the same gentle way that Jesus does.

By the end of the day, you're anxious to have Jesus as a companion for the next day. So you ask Him, "Do you think You could stay with me a while?"

"Well," He replies, "My plan is to sit here all night and watch you while you sleep. That's one of My favorite things to do. And tomorrow, if you want, we can do this again."[4]

Now, doesn't that kind of an adventure with God sound like fun? Give it a shot today. You may well feel His guidance in specific ways—perhaps in what to eat or drink or wear—but it's a leading couched in a friendship, not some arbitrary celestial secretive "will" that He is hiding from you and it's your job to solve the mystery and figure out His plan. When it comes to bigger decisions in life—whom to marry, what career to choose, how many kids to have, and so on—you approach it the same way. Carry on a continual conversation with Jesus and make your choices accordingly. Base your decisions on a daily friendship with the Maker of the stars, rather than on their alignment.

In this way, you give God your will. Ellen White offers this insight:

"Many are inquiring, '*How* am I to make the surrender of myself to God?' You desire to give yourself to Him, but you are weak in moral power, in slavery to doubt, and controlled by the habits of your life of sin. Your promises and resolutions are like ropes of sand. You cannot control your thoughts, your impulses, your affections. The knowledge of your broken promises and forfeited pledges weakens your confidence in your own sincerity, and causes you to feel that God cannot accept you; but you need not despair. What you need to understand is the true force of the will. This is the governing power in the nature of man, the power of decision, or of choice. Everything depends on the right action of the will. The power of choice God has given to men; it is theirs to exercise. You cannot change your heart, you cannot of yourself give to God its affections; but you can *choose* to serve Him. You can give Him your will; He will then work in you to will and to do according to His good pleasure. Thus your whole nature will be brought under the control of the Spirit of Christ; your affections will be centered upon Him, your thoughts will be in harmony with Him."[5]

What About Faith?

Perhaps you find yourself on the outskirts of faith. Maybe you were born into a religious tradition but you wrestle with the relevance of it all. Does God really care if you attend church? Is that part of His purpose in your life? Isn't it enough to forge your own pathway to God? After all, aren't we all going to the same place? How are we to understand the oppression and violence that has scarred our world, all in the name of God and His church? And what do we do with all the hypocrisy in the church? Must I really belong to such a tainted community of faith?

It is unquestionably true that hypocrisy, violence, and all manner of evil have flourished in the church. Yet it is equally true that the church has historically been responsible for building some of the finest hospitals, schools, orphanages, and senior-care facilities, and some of the most compassionate communities, in the world. When I am asked, "How do you defend the Crusades or the Inquisition or the burning of witches or modern-day evils such as sexual abuse or financial fraud committed by leaders in the church?" my answer is simple: "I don't defend any such sin." I would respond with a question of my own: "When people who claim to be followers of Christ do evil things, is it *because* of His teachings, or is it *in spite* of them?"

It is impossible to read the Sermon on the Mount in Matthew 5 through 7 and defend abuse, hypocrisy, or any manner of evil. How can anyone argue that Jesus commissioned the atrocities committed in His name? After all, He said, "You have heard that it was said, 'Love your neighbor and hate your enemy.' But I tell you, love your enemies and pray for those who persecute you, that you may be children of your Father in heaven" (Matt. 5:43-45). No such creative exegetical gymnastics will permit us to interpret such teachings as a license to kill or harm others.

I won't argue that the church is perfect. In the next chapter we'll further explore the importance of the church, but here we must acknowledge that every congregation is packed with perverts, hypocrites, liars, addicts, cheats, and vegetarians who eat people. I will contend, though, that God calls every one of His kids to belong to His beloved church. The church is His bride, His body, and the manifestation of Himself on earth. Thus it is part of God's purpose for all of His cherished children to belong. You see, it is not enough to just believe, or even just to behave; God makes it clear that you belong on this earth. To that end He calls you to be a part of His community—the church.

Paul compliments the Macedonian churches by describing them in this way:

"They gave themselves first of all to the Lord, and then by the will of God also to us" (2 Cor. 8:5).

Faith begins by giving yourself fully to God. Then it finds meaning and context in God's church. This is the "will of God."

"Each one of you is part of the body of Christ," Paul teaches, "and you were chosen to live together in peace" (Col. 3:15, CEV). Did you catch that? You are a "part of the body of Christ." "You were chosen." You matter.

A few years ago my body told me that I was too old to play in the local college football league, but I wanted to believe that I was the same carefree jock I had been 20 years earlier. Then one night I was reminded again why I have no business sharing a football field with guys half my age and twice my speed.

"You OK?" the student (who had just blown by me doing Mach 2) asked.

"Oh yeah," I shrugged. "I just caught my finger in your flag belt and twisted it. I'm sure it will be fine by the end of the game. You had a nice run."

But by the end of the game my pinky was throbbing. The only problem was that Walla Walla had no walk-in clinics open at 10:00 p.m.; my only option was the emergency room. That felt like overkill, but my finger hurt. So my friend Troy drove me to the hospital (given the serious injury, you wouldn't expect me to drive myself, would you?). I marched past the flashing lights, wailing sirens, and scurrying paramedics to the receptionist.

"Excuse me," I said.

"Yes, and what is your emergency?"

I wanted to display a bullet wound in my arm or leg, or complain of a broken back, but instead I mumbled, "Um, ah, my pinky hurts."

An hour later the doctor pointed to a line on the X-ray and said, "You definitely broke your finger. You can see the fracture in the bone right there."

"Hallelujah!" I squealed. "It's a bona fide sports injury. You better give me a full body cast!" After all, you can never be too careful when it comes to serious accidents.

"I think a finger splint might work better," the doctor smirked.

"Very well. I'm just glad you found something wrong. I didn't want to explain to all my friends that I was rushed to the emergency room just for a pinky pain. A 'broken bone' sounds more legit."

One lesson that incident taught me was the value of every pinky. While it may not be the most visible part of the body or the most used, the pinky is nonetheless a vital part. If you don't believe that, break your pinky and try typing this chapter. Be sure to budget twice the time it normally takes. Believe it or not, your pinky is critical.

When it comes to the body, God didn't make spare parts. Every part matters.

And the same applies to the body of Christ—His church. God didn't make spare parts. Again, every part matters.

As a pastor I've often reminded people of this. A conversation comes to mind with a young woman who cried, "I don't have anything to contribute to the church."

"Nonsense," I said. "What do you love to do?"

"If I told you, you'd laugh."

"Try me."

"Well, what I really love is writing poetry."

I laughed and said, "Oh, well, there's no place for you in the ch—" No! I didn't say any such thing. "Then write poetry," I actually replied. "Write me a poem on the Second Coming, and I'll use it in my next sermon." She crafted a masterpiece—the first of many of her poems I used to punctuate my sermons.

Whether you're a math whiz, sculptor, flutist, mechanic, computer expert, or poet, God can use your creative gifts. That's why He gave them to you. So unleash the creative genius in you. You are a vital part of God's community. To squelch your creativity is to break a bone in the body of Christ. Now, that's a *real* emergency.

---

[1] Donald Miller, "Does God Have a Specific Plan for Your Life? Probably Not," Apr. 29, 2010, http://donmilleris.com/2010/04/29/does-god-have-a-specific-plan-for-your-life-probably-not/ (accessed Mar. 12, 2012).

[2] *Ibid.*

[3] Ellen G. White, *Selected Messages* (Washington, D.C.: Review and Herald Pub. Assn., 1958, 1980), book 2, pp. 16, 17.

[4] Adapted from sermon cassette C0028, by John Ortberg, "How to Spend a Day With Jesus" (South Barrington, Ill.: Willow Creek Community Church).

[5] Ellen G. White, *Steps to Christ* (Mountain View, Calif.: Pacific Press Pub. Assn., 1956), p. 47.

Church Matters

Since my favorite café opened at 6:30 this Sunday morning, I've had the joint all to myself. For more than an hour I've claimed my nook, spreading books and notes all over a long table for six. I was writing this chapter when an African-American man walked in, stepped to the counter, and placed his order. He caught my eye because he looked as though he was heading to an NFL team owners meeting: silk hat, pinstriped suit, glittering gold globs on more fingers than not, patterned shirt with a perfectly placed tie and hanky that impeccably accented the outfit, and shoes that warned that I should don sunglasses before staring directly at them.

To say he seemed the chatty type is like suggesting Donald Trump seems the confident type. While they stirred up his order he bubbled with way more energy than any human should have at that hour of the morning.

"I missed you yesterday," he said to the barista. "Yep, I couldn't come by to see you, but ain't no way I was going to miss two days in a row. But how 'bout this weather we're enjoying? Sure hope you're having a blessed day."

The place had 10 tables, but where did he want to sit? You got it—at *my* table. Inching my nose closer to the screen, I wanted to make it real clear that I am a working man, intent on my book, my thoughts, my world.

"Good morning. You having a blessed day?" he asked.

I typed wildly, pretending that he must be talking to someone else. Problem was, nobody else was there.

"Good morning; how are you?" he persisted.

He acted as if we were old college roommates while I tried to communicate that I wanted to get this chapter written.

"You working on a book or something?"

OK, there was no ducking this conversation. "Yes." I reluctantly lifted my gaze.

"I'm on my way to church," he enthused before sipping his coffee. The only stimulant in this man was clearly the Spirit. "But the church is no building," he replied, starting to wind up like a televangelist. "Oh, no! The church is not stone or mortar or pulpit or pew. It is Jesus, crucified, resurrected, glorified, and personalized in His people, for His people, through His people, sanctified for His purpose, in His power, polished with His poise, and persistent in His passion . . . "

I braced myself for an offering appeal. "You're on your way to church?"

"Yes sir," he grinned. "I'm Reverend Abraham Jackson, pastor at Joshua Christian Ministries. Are you a believer as well?"

"Yes," I answered, guessing that I had just foiled a sermon illustration for him. "In fact, I'm also a pastor . . . and an author."

We had chatted for 15 minutes or so when it occurred to me that rather than seeing this guy as an impediment to my writing, I could enlist him as a partner. So I said, "I'm working on a book right now and was wondering what you would say to the young skeptic who believes something like this: 'There is no absolute truth. We will all reach our destiny by different roads, but we're going to the same place. So you don't need Jesus or His church. In fact, the church is irrelevant—and certainly unnecessary for salvation. Spirituality is an individual journ—'"

As I suspected, he was happy to preach it from there. "I would say to that person that there is only one way to heaven and that is through Jeeeeeeeee-sus Christ. As for the church, it is Christ's body on this earth. Every believer is called to belong to Christ's church. Why, we were created for community, called for caring, christened for compassion . . . "

The Church

He kept going, but I got the quote I wanted: "Every believer is called to belong to Christ's church." Indeed, the church is Christ's body on earth. The apostle Paul explains, "For just as each of us has one body with many members, and these members do not all have the same function, so in Christ we, though many, form one body, and each member belongs to all the others" (Rom. 12:4, 5).

Jesus calls each of us to "belong" to the church. By "church" we're not talking about a program or a building; rather, we're talking about Christ's people—His body. Now, for a body to be robust and healthy, every organ must perform its purpose. Similarly, if you want to be strong and healthy, then you must function in the body according to your called purpose. Simply put, you can't fulfill your God-ordained destiny if you are disconnected from His community.

Malcolm Gladwell, in his book *Outliers*, tells the bizarre story of Christopher Langan, a genius with a staggering IQ of 195 (compared to Einstein's IQ of 150). During high school Langan could ace any foreign language test by skimming the textbook three minutes before the exam. He got a perfect score on his SAT, even though at one point he fell asleep. But Langan has never fully used his exceptional intellect. He currently owns and operates a horse ranch in rural Missouri.

According to Gladwell, Langan never had a community to help him make the most of his gifts. Gladwell summarizes the story of Langan in one sentence: "[Langan] had to make his way alone, and no one—not rock stars, not professional athletes, not software billionaires, and not even geniuses—ever makes it alone."[1]

If you're serious about fulfilling your destiny and reaching your God-ordained potential, then you cannot go it alone. You belong. God called and uniquely gifted you to contribute to a community bigger than just yourself.

For better or worse, the community that God designed for us is His church. We're an imperfect people to be sure, trying to find our way in this world while on our way to the next. And we admittedly don't have everything figured out. The debates rage relative to the church:

Is the church irrelevant in today's post-modern world?

Does the "emerging church" create a promising bridge between God and culture? Or is it really a bridge between believers and compromise?

How can we safeguard a personal walk with God and remain faithful in the wider context of church?

Such questions deserve thoughtful consideration well beyond the scope of this book, but for our purposes let's at least dip our toes into the muddy spiritual waters.

The [Ir]Relevancy of the Church

So is the church losing its relevancy? *USA Today* reports:

"Bye-bye, church. We're busy." That's the message teens are giving churches today.

"Only about one in four teens now participate in church youth groups, considered the hallmark of involvement; numbers have been flat since 1999. Other measures of religiosity—prayer, Bible reading, and going to church—lag as well, according to the Barna Group, a Ventura, California, evangelical research company. This all has churches canceling their summer teen camps and youth pastors looking worriedly toward the fall, when school-year youth groups kick in.

" 'Talking to God may be losing out to Facebook,' says Barna president David Kinnaman.

" 'Sweet 16 is not a sweet spot for churches. It's the age teens typically drop out,' says Thom Rainer, president of LifeWay Christian Resources, Nashville, Tennessee, which found the turning point in a study of church dropouts. 'A decade ago teens were coming to church youth group to play, coming for the entertainment, coming for the pizza. They're not even coming for the pizza anymore. They say, "We don't see the church as relevant, as meeting our needs or where we need to be today." ' "[2]

What do you reckon? Should we be concerned? After all, if the church plays prominently into the conversation about purpose, calling, and destiny, shouldn't its ailing vitals give us cause for alert?

The Emerging Church

Many church members are deeply concerned—so much so that they are actively shaping answers. The result is what scholars have labeled as "the emerging church."

Wikipedia.com gives this definition to it: "A Christian movement of the late twentieth and early twenty-first century that crosses a number of theological boundaries: participants can be described as Protestant, post-Protestant, Catholic, evangelical, post-evangelical, liberal, post-liberal, conservative, post-conservative, neocharismatic, and post-charismatic. Proponents, however, believe the movement transcends such 'modernist' labels of 'conservative' and 'liberal,' calling the movement a 'conversation' to emphasize its developing and decentralized nature, its vast range of standpoints, and its commitment to dialogue. Participants seek to live their faith in what they believe to be a 'postmodern' society. What those involved in the conversation mostly agree on is their disillusionment with the organized and institutional church and their support for the deconstruction of modern Christian worship, modern evangelism, and the nature of modern Christian community."[3]

John Jovan Markovic, professor of modern European and church history and a researcher on the topic of Emergent spirituality, writes: "The spine of the Emergent paradigm of thinking, or the Emergent matrix of reality, is 'both/and' rather than the traditional Western 'either/or.' The Emergents refuse to separate reality. The very notion of emerging is to accept the idea that all voices need to be heard, that all narratives (stories) need to be told, and that whatever emerges out of it all is the Emergent metanarrative—if there is such a thing. No individual and no group can have a metanarrative that dominates all the others. According to this thinking, the biblical great conflict narrative between Christ and Satan, between good and evil, is pushed to the side, ignored, or downplayed. It is misinterpreted as intolerant, judgmental, divisive, repulsive, and nonapplicable to contemporary social needs. It should be of no surprise that the Emergents have a difficult time dealing with the subjects of atonement and the destruction of sinners. [4]

While it's impossible to agree on an exact definition of emerging churches, they tend to place a high value on:

» Dialoguing with people holding a postmodernism worldview.
» Using technology in a creative way.
» Experiencing sensory worship using candles, icons, images, sounds, and smells.
» Teaching inclusive, sometimes contradictory, beliefs.
» Emphasizing experience and feelings above absolutes.
» Replacing stale traditionalism in worship, church seating, and music with contemporary forms.
» Downplaying absolutes and doctrinal creeds.
» Repositioning the Christian church in society.
» Reexamining the Bible and its teachings.
» Reevaluating traditional doctrines.

While such values have much to admire, there always exists the potential of straying from biblical, Christocentric teaching in the interest of relevancy. Now, of course, churches carrying the "emergent" tag vary greatly in theology and practice. It would be inaccurate and unwise to dismiss all "emergent churches" as feel-good fellowships of inclusivism that worship Allah, Buddha, God, and Tim Tebow. We dare not be close-minded to a fresh expression of God's Spirit sweeping through His church. Nor should we be equally reckless to the other extreme and make no distinction between right and wrong. All churches are *not* created equal.

The Church "In" Not "Of"
We must find that delicate balance between uncompromising truth

and unapologetic relevancy. The clearest picture we have of such balance is in Jesus.

He was uncompromising in speaking truth. He boldly proclaimed, "I am . . . the truth" (John 14:6). He didn't say, "I am one of many viable truths," but rather, "*the* truth." As edgy, offensive and politically incorrect as it sounds, there is such a thing as sin. Moral absolutes do exist, creating right and wrong. And there is only one way to salvation—Jesus Christ.

He was also relevant to His culture. The crowds flocked to Him because He spoke their language, attended their weddings, healed their hurts, and shared their meals.

Jesus prayed that we would find the same balance between being *in* the world but not *of* the world:

"I am coming to you now, but I say these things while I am still in the world, so that they may have the full measure of my joy within them. I have given them your word and the world has hated them, for they are not of the world any more than I am of the world. My prayer is not that you take them out of the world but that you protect them from the evil one. They are not of the world, even as I am not of it. Sanctify them by the truth; your word is truth. As you sent me into the world, I have sent them into the world" (John 17:13-18).

I like J. Wilbur Chapman's interpretation of Jesus' prayer: "It's not the ship in the water but the water in the ship that sinks it. So it's not the Christian in the world but the world in the Christian that constitutes the danger."

The guiding principle here suggests that Christians should separate themselves from sinful *pursuits*, not from sinful *people*. Luke 19:10 offers Jesus as our example:

"For the Son of Man came to seek and to save the lost."

Remember how the religious leaders got in a tizzy because Jesus befriended sinners? They kept muttering, "This man welcomes sinners and eats with them" (Luke 15:2). Jesus did not engage in sinful activities, but He loved sinners. So, too, we must separate ourselves from sinful activity—not from sinful people.

Many years ago I was a student working on my M.B.A. at a university in Seattle. Just as I was finishing up that program I accepted a call to move to Walla Walla. After class one evening a classmate cornered me and said, "I hear you're moving to Walla Walla."

"You've heard of it?" I was surprised.

"I used to live there," she explained. "Well, actually we lived in a suburb of Walla Walla."

Now I was really amused. I didn't think Walla Walla was big enough to have its own suburb. "Yes," she said, "we lived in a town called College Place."

"What was that like?" I asked.

She said, "It's a nice little community. There are a lot of Adventists there. Everyone in our cul-de-sac was an Adventist."

"Really? What's an Adventist?"

"Well, I think it's like a church or something. They're nice enough people, but the only thing I know about them is that they never do garage sales on Saturday. Isn't that weird?"

"Really?"

Then she asked me, "So why are you moving there?"

"It's a job transfer."

"What kind of work do you do?"

How is my work any of her business? "Well, um," I stammered, "I'm . . . an Adventist pastor."

"Really?" she exclaimed. "You are a pastor? I had no idea. You seem so . . . normal."

That conversation still haunts me. How is it that a woman can live in a neighborhood comprised only of Seventh-day Adventist Christians and yet years later the only thing she knows about Adventists is that they don't do garage sales on Saturday? It makes me wonder if we are becoming that "irrelevant church" we read about in the newspaper.

Jesus is calling you to be a part of His church on this earth. We're not a perfect community, nor are we always relevant to the world. But as blemished and irrelevant and offensive as we might be, we are still the bride of Jesus, waiting for the Bridegroom to take us home. Never forget:

"Christ loved the church and gave himself up for her to make her holy, cleansing her by the washing with water through the word, and to present her to himself as a radiant church, without stain or wrinkle or any other blemish, but holy and blameless" (Eph. 5:25-27).

---

[1] Malcolm Gladwell, *Outliers* (New York: Little, Brown and Co., 2008), p. 115.

[2] Cathy Lynn Grossman and Stephanie Steinberg, "'Forget Pizza Parties,' Teens Tell Churches," *USA Today*, Dec. 11, 2010, www.usatoday.com/news/religion/2010-08-11-teenchurch11_ST_N.htm (accessed Mar. 19, 2012).

[3] http://en.wikipedia.org/wiki/The_Emerging_Church (accessed Mar. 19, 2012).

[4] John Jovan Markovic, "The Emerging Church: A Call to Action and Authenticity," *Ministry*, March 2010.

Where **Am I Going?**

"I can't change the direction of the wind,
but I can adjust my sails to always reach my destination."

—Jimmy Dean

"From eternal ages it was God's purpose that every created being,
from bright and holy seraph to man,
should be a temple for the indwelling of the Creator."

—Ellen G. White

"I know where I'm going and I know the truth,
and I don't have to be what you want me to be.
I'm free to be what I want."

—Muhammad Ali

"We dwell on the past,
and worry about the future;
we exist in life and forget to live."

—Samuel Richardson

YOU:
On a Tombstone

Doctors Michael Roizen and Mehmet Oz have struck gold with their wildly popular book series *YOU*. The initial one, *YOU: The Owner's Manual*, was the first book to dethrone Harry Potter, who had dominated the number one spot on the New York *Times* best seller list for five months. Since then they have written numerous sequels: *YOU: The Smart Patient; YOU: Staying Young; YOU: On a Walk; YOU: Breathing Easy; YOU: Being Beautiful; YOU: Having a Baby; YOU: The Owner's Manual for Teens; Tu, a dieta: Manual de instrucciones para reducir tu cintura*—all of them best sellers.

Upon release of their sixth book, *YOU: On a Diet,* they appeared on *Oprah*. It was one of her highest rated shows of all time. The book debuted at number one on the best seller list, selling 2.4 million copies in the first three weeks.

Not that they are calling my agent (and not that I have an agent), but I would love to contribute to their book series. My title would be *YOU: On a Tombstone*. It would have four chapters.

Chapter One: Date of Birth

The first chapter marks the date of your birth. Almost every tombstone notes when that particular person was born. In this chapter I would underscore the biblical teaching that your birth was no accident. God created you for a purpose. You are unique, and there is nobody else on the planet like you.

The psalmist declared to God: "For you created my inmost being; you knit me together in my mother's womb. I praise you because I am fearfully and wonderfully made; your works are wonderful, I know that full well. My frame was not hidden from you when I was made in the secret place, when I was woven together in the depths of the earth. Your eyes saw my unformed body, all the days ordained for me were written in your book before one of them came to be" (Ps. 139:13-16).

God's message to you: "Before I formed you in the womb I knew you, before you were born I set you apart; I appointed you as a prophet to the nations" (Jer. 1:5).

The Lord will never miss your birthday party. He celebrates you! In God's mind you are flawless.

From a human perspective a life may be scorned—even destroyed. Using our cruel, arbitrary metrics, we measure the value of a human being on such phony criterion as color of skin, height, weight, talent, and so on. But God will have nothing to do with those standards. In every child God marvels at His masterpiece.

Dr. Frederic Loomis grappled with God's view of every child. He faced the most difficult decision that a physician could ever make—whether to allow a deformed baby to live or die. He had only seconds to decide.

While Loomis had delivered hundreds of babies, this one was different. The infant lay in a breech position, promising at best a difficult and dangerous birth. One of its feet stretched only to the knee of the other leg. Furthermore, it was missing a thigh. The mother, a frail person visiting the sterile delivery room for her first time, was not aware of the grossly deformed child struggling to survive.

Closing his eyes, the physician thought, *Would not the most loving thing be to detain the birth long enough to cause the child to be stillborn?* He agonized within himself. *Will this kid not be considered a freak, a twisted burden to its delicate mother? How can I justify playing a part in such a cruel drama? Surely no one will ever know if I spare this family inevitable pain.*

The doctor, through the baby's cord, felt its heartbeat—dancing in rhythm to his own wildly racing heart. As Loomis continued to prevent the birth, he felt the normal foot pressing for passage into the world. Suddenly he could no longer justify "playing God." Instead, he would trust the Lord to care for this child against what seemed to be impossible odds. He delivered the infant into the world, which, he sensed, would be very unkind.

In the years that followed, Loomis often second-guessed his decision while he watched the anguish of the family as the desperate parents sought in vain to find some correction for their child's deformity. Even after they moved away he continued to lament the burden that he had saddled upon the family. Their heartache, he often told himself, was his fault.

In time, however, Dr. Loomis would find peace. It came at an unexpected time and place—the hospital Christmas party. Typically it was during the holiday season that his pain seemed most severe. He could not shake the image of that unfortunate child from his mind. While the world celebrated the greatest birth ever known, Loomis obsessed about the saddest birth he had ever experienced. At this particular party the most heavenly music filled the room. The sadness seemed to dissipate as the rich tones of "Silent Night" washed his anguished spirit.

Following the concert, a woman approached him. "Doctor," she said excitedly, "You saw her."

Loomis studied the woman's face, wanting to recognize her but unable to recall the memory. "I'm sorry. I should know you, but you may need to help me."

"Don't you remember the little girl with only one good leg, 17 years ago?"

Remember! It was the one thing in his life that he couldn't forget! In disbelief he listened to her story. "That baby was my daughter, Doctor. And I saw you watching her play the harp tonight! She has an artificial leg. She's doing well."

At her mom's bidding, the lovely harpist walked toward them. Dr. Loomis enveloped the girl in his arms. "Please," he said in a tightening voice, "please play 'Silent Night' for me one more time."

The young woman hobbled to her harp and played his request with poise and perfection. As she did, he reflected on the incredible gift of life. He thought about the sanctity in every person. And he exhaled 17 years of questions and wondering whether or not it was wise to grant a baby life.[1]

Every child is created in the image of God.

Chapter Two: Dash

The second chapter in our book is the humble dash. That "—" separates the bookends of your life on earth. This tiny symbol captures your journey from diapers to hospice.

That dash is so short, isn't it? "What is your dash?" James wonders. Then he answers: "You are a mist that appears for a little while and then vanishes" (James 4:14).

Blink, and your dash is over.

Recently I was on an airplane when I had an opportunity to practice my primary spiritual gift: eavesdropping. I was tuning in to a conversation between two elderly women who I guessed were pushing 80. It was apparent by their conversation that they had connections with the airline, so they were free to travel as much as they liked.

Then one of them said something that nearly kicked me into cardiac arrest. The woman said, "I'm just heading to Pittsburgh for the weekend to attend my 30-year high school reunion."

I choked, deeply offended. Why? Because I was flying to *my* 30-year high school reunion as well! As I stared at her the terrifying thought assaulted me: *I am as old as that ancient woman.*

I tried to misconstrue the obvious. *She probably attended high school in her 30s . . . I jog every day, so I don't look that old . . . Maybe she said, "I went to high school in 1930."*

Oh, I tried to spin the facts. But no amount of mental wizardry could help me to escape the truth: I am getting old. Fast.

And so are you.

The dash is so short. Lewis Smedes reminds us of this fact:

"I bought a brand-new date book yesterday, the kind I use every year—spiral-bound, black imitation leather covers wrapped around pages and pages of blank boxes. Every square has a number to tell me which day of the month I'm in at the moment. Every square is a frame for one episode of my life. Before I'm through with the book, I will fill the squares with classes I teach, people with whom I ate lunch, everlasting committee meetings I sit through, and these are only the things I cannot afford to forget. I fill the squares too with things I do not write down to remember: thousands of cups of coffee, some lovemaking, some praying, and, I hope, gestures of help to my neighbors. Whatever I do, it has to fit inside one of those squares on my date book. I live one square at a time. The four lines that make up the box are the walls of time that organize my life. Each box has an invisible door that leads to the next square. As if by a silent stroke, the door opens and I am pulled through, as if by a magnet, sucked into the next square in line. There I will again fill the time frame that seals me—fill it with my busyness just as I did the square before. As I get older, the squares seem to get smaller. One day I will walk into a square that has no door. There will be no mysterious opening and walking into an adjoining square. One of those squares will be terminal. I do not know which square it will be."

As it turned out, Smedes entered that last square on December 19, 2002. He died from complications after a fall at his home in California.

Robert Brault rightly observes, "Life is short, God's way of encouraging a bit of focus."

So what is the focus of your life?

Peter reminds us that our time on this earth is brief. "The end of all things is near," he writes. "Therefore . . . love each other deeply, because love covers over a multitude of sins. Offer hospitality to one another without grumbling. Each of you should use whatever gift you have received to serve others, as faithful stewards of God's grace in its various forms" (1 Peter 4:7-10).

Use your short dash to be a steward of God's grace. Love. Give. Serve. No matter your age, social standing, spiritual gifts, or circumstances in life, you can be a difference-maker with your dash.

When my daughter Lindsey was 14, she attended a Youth Specialties Convention, at which she heard a young woman share her testimony of growing up homeless in the Bronx, New York. The speaker had quite the impact. Lindsey came home and said, "Dad, did you know there are kids in the Bronx who can't get a decent meal and who don't have a place to sleep at night?"

"I'm sure that's true," I agreed with her. "It's very sad."

"Well, Dad," she insisted, "we've got to do something to help."

"Honey, that's a great idea," I brushed her off. But that conversation was far from over.

Day after day Lindsey insisted, "Dad, we've got to help those people in the Bronx."

"Good idea," I agreed in a patronizing tone.

Lindsey was determined. She started asking her friends, "Did you know there are kids who are homeless and hungry in the Bronx? Will you come with me to help them?"

"Yeah, that's a great idea," they agreed.

Then I got the invitation. "Dad, you want to go on a mission trip to New York City for spring break?"

"You can't just go to New York for spring break," I said.

"Why not?"

"Well, you don't drive. And that will cost a lot of money. And you don't know anybody in New York City—where are you going to stay and what are you going to do?"

A few days later a church member at the office stopped me. "Hey, Pastor, you coming with us on our mission trip to the Bronx?"

"Huh?"

"Yeah, did you know there are homeless and hungry kids in the Bronx? We need to do something about that, don't you think?"

"Well, yes, but . . ."

It was time for a "Come to Jesus" talk with my daughter. "Lindsey," I said sternly, "you can't be announcing a mission trip to the Bronx when you don't have a clue how you're going to get there, what you're going to do when you're there, where you're going to stay, or how you're going to pay for it. How are you going to pull this off?"

"I dunno," she shrugged. "That's God's problem."

"How are you going to get there?"

"Don't you want to come?"

"Well, we can't afford to take our family to New York City for spring break. That would be thousands of dollars. Where's that money going to come from?"

"That's God's problem, not mine. I just know God wants us to go help the homeless and hungry kids in the Bronx."

"But Lindsey, you can't just say God will pay for it . . ."

"But Dad, isn't that what you preach about—that we're supposed to step out in faith when God tells us to do something?" (I hate it when my kids preach *my* sermons to me. There must be a text in the Bible somewhere that says they shouldn't do that!)

"Well, no, yes, um, it's not exactly the same," I stammered. "We can't afford to do this."

She calmly replied, "God will figure it out."

The following weekend I spoke at a church in northern California. When I arrived, I met one of the church members there who handed me an envelope. I could see it was a check.

"What is this?" I asked.

"It's a little something that I want you to use for a mission of your choice. I know you don't charge an honorarium, but this isn't an honorarium. We want you to put this into a mission trip."

Later when I opened the envelope my heart about stopped. It contained a check for thousands of dollars—plenty of coin to cover our mission trip to the Bronx. I wondered if Lindsey had called the church and posed as my booking agent: "You can pay Dr. Haffner's speaker's fee upon his arrival, right?" No, she didn't do that. But it sure felt suspicious.

I couldn't wait to get home to share the good news with her. Elated, albeit not overly surprised, she had known that God would provide a way for our family to serve the hungry and homeless kids in the Bronx.

The following month our family joined several other families to serve at the Love Kitchen in the Bronx. We volunteered at the Latino Community Center and helped the children at a day-care center in the Bronx. After sleeping on a gym floor, we took icy cold showers, then worked 12-hour days. And it was the best spring break ever.

The whole deal happened because of a 14-year-old kid who believed God was calling her to help hungry and homeless kids in the Bronx. Whether you are 14 or 114, you can make a difference with your dash. God is calling you to fill every little square of your short life with acts of love that others will remember long after your chapter on earth has ended.

Chapter Three: Date of Death

In short order we come to the third chapter of our book *YOU: On a Tombstone*. It marks the date of death. Solomon speaks of the inevitability of death in Ecclesiastes 9:10:

"Whatever your hand finds to do, do it with all your might, for in the realm of the dead, where you are going, there is neither working nor planning nor knowledge nor wisdom."

The Bible is clear: You and I are going to the grave. Contemporary philosopher Simon Critchley, in *The Book of Dead Philosophers*, explores the deaths and the teachings about death attributed to 190 great thinkers of the past. Many of the stories are downright bizarre: Heracleitus suffocated in cow dung; Aristotle reportedly committed suicide by swallowing aconite; Empedocles, according to legend, plunged into Mount Etna aspiring to become a god; Jeremy Bentham had himself stuffed and sits on public display at University College, London.

Critchley notes with a tinge of acerbity that even Christians are afraid to die:

"A detailed national survey . . . from 2003 claimed that fully 92 percent of Americans believe in God, 85 percent believe in heaven, and 82 percent believe in miracles. But the deeper truth is that such religious belief, complete with a heavenly afterlife, brings believers little solace in relation to death. The only priesthood in which people *really* believe is the medical profession and the purpose of their sacramental drugs and technology is to support longevity, the sole unquestioned good of contemporary Western life.

"If proof were needed that many religious believers actually do not practice what they preach, then it can be found in the ignorance of religious teaching on death, particularly Christian teaching. . . . Christianity, in the hands of a Paul, an Augustine or a Luther, is a way of becoming reconciled to the brevity of human life and giving up the desire for wealth, worldly goods, and temporal power. . . . [But many Christians today] are actually leading desperate atheist lives bounded by a desire for longevity and a terror of [death]."[2]

Could Critchley be right? Are Christians simply masked atheists who desperately embrace a particular worldview to anesthetize a frantic fear of dying? Perhaps Christians are like Arthur Miller, the playwright, who died on February 10, 2005. When he was asked about writing his own epitaph, he claimed he had never given it any thought. Then he added, "I expect to be here indefinitely."[3]

I guess Miller missed the boat on that one, huh? Scripture affirms that indeed we will all die.

"All people are like grass," Isaiah declares, "and all their faithfulness is like the flowers of the field. The grass withers and the flowers fall, because the breath of the Lord blows on them. Surely the people are grass. The grass withers and the flowers fall" (Isa. 40:6-8).

"Like water spilled on the ground, which cannot be recovered, so we must die," 2 Samuel 14:14 explains. The text goes on, however, to convey this hope: "But that is not what God desires; rather, he devises ways so that a banished person does not remain banished from him."

Indeed, we do not need to fear death, for we share a hope that we will be reunited with God for eternity. We are not just here for a spit and that's that; life is more than a short party on earth. I am reminded of the story shared by Nancy Walker of Newport Beach, California. Her 5-year-old neighbor, Jimmy Yeargan, invited her to attend the funeral of his goldfish. Since Jimmy was not yet able to write at the time, he asked Walker to do the honors for him, handing her a small, cardboard tombstone that he had brought with him to the ceremony.

"What do you want to say?" she asked.

"His name," Jimmy replied, "was Mobert." Dutifully Ms. Walker inscribed the name.

"Do you want anything else?" she asked. Jimmy thought for a moment, then nodded.

"Yes," he said, "please write, 'He was fun while he lasted.'"

Is that a fitting epitaph? "Fun while he lasted"—but beyond a few giggles, well, there's not much more to the story. So is that really it? No!

Good news! There is one more chapter to my book, *YOU: On A Tombstone.*

Chapter Four: An Exclamation Point

The final chapter is no bigger in size than the dash—it is an exclamation point. By this symbol I would hope to convey the good news that our story does not end with the date of death. The apostle Paul offers this hope:

"Brothers and sisters, we do not want you to be uninformed about those who sleep in death, so that you do not grieve like the rest of mankind, who have no hope. For we believe that Jesus died and rose again, and so we believe that God will bring with Jesus those who have fallen asleep in him. According to the Lord's word, we tell you that we who are still alive, who are left until the coming of the Lord, will certainly not precede those who have fallen asleep. For the Lord himself will come down from heaven, with a loud command, with the voice of the archangel and with the trumpet call of God, and the dead in Christ will rise first. After that, we who are still alive and are left will be caught up together with them in the clouds to meet the Lord in the air. And so we will be with the Lord forever. Therefore encourage one another with these words" (1 Thess. 4:13-18).

For Christians the story does not close with death. Jesus conquered the grave, and because He exploded out of the tomb we can engrave a bold exclamation point upon our tombstone in the sure and final hope that someday, God will set things right. Then there will be no more cancer, no more tears, no more death. And we will be with the Lord forever!

---

[1] www.crossroad.to/Victory/stories/image.htm (accessed Mar. 9, 2012).

[2] Simon Critchley, *The Book of Dead Philosophers* (New York: Vintage Books, 2008), pp. 247, 248.

[3] *CBS Evening News*, Feb. 11, 2005.

Blessed Assurance

Velma Barfield, a victim of incest as a child, was a woman from rural North Carolina. In 1978 she was arrested for murdering four people, including her mother and fiancé. Admitting her guilt, she shared the chilling story of her drug-crazed life, beginning with tranquilizers that her doctor prescribed following a painful injury.

As she sat in solitary confinement one night, the guard tuned in to a 24-hour gospel station. Down the gray hall, desperate and alone in her cell, Velma heard the words of an evangelist and asked Jesus Christ to take over her life. She wrote, "I had been in and out of churches all my life, and I could explain all about God. But I had never understood before that Jesus had died for me."

Her conversion seemed genuine. For six years on death row she ministered to many of her cellmates. The outside world began to hear about Velma Barfield. As the story of her remarkable rehabilitation became known, God used Velma's cell on death row as a pulpit.

Before her final sentence, Velma wrote to a friend:

"If I am executed on August 31, I know the Lord will give me dying grace, just as He gave me saving grace, and has given me living grace."

Velma Barfield was the first woman in 22 years to be executed in the United States. She lingered in the valley of the shadow of death for many years. At her memorial service Pastor Hugh Hoyle said, "She died with dignity, and she died with purpose. Velma is a living demonstration of 'by the grace of God you shall be saved.'"[1]

Bad News/Good News

Whether it's a murderer, a molester, or me, on the day of judgment we all deserve the same punishment. We all sit on death row in the eternal scheme. Like Velma, our choices condemn us. And the Bible is clear: "The wages of sin is death" (Rom. 6:23). That's the bad news.

The good news declares, "But the gift of God is eternal life in Christ Jesus our Lord." Because Jesus sits in our electric chair, we escape death and receive life. Like Velma, we too can die "with purpose," demonstrating God's grace. Just live in Jesus, and you have no reason to fear the judgment.

As Frederick Buechner once said: "The New Testament proclaims that at some unforeseeable time in the future, God will ring down the final curtain on history, and there will come a Day on which all our days and all the judgments upon us and all our judgments upon each other will themselves be judged. The judge will be Christ. In other words, the one who judges us most finally will be the one who loves us most fully."[2]

Paul declares in Ephesians: "For it is by God's grace that you have been saved through faith. It is not the result of your own efforts, but God's gift" (Eph. 2:8, 9, TEV).

Ellen White explains: "We must behold Christ. It is ignorance of Him that makes men so uplifted in their own righteousness. When we contemplate His purity and excellence, we shall see our own weakness and poverty and defects as they really are. We shall see ourselves lost and hopeless, clad in garments of self-righteousness, like every other sinner. We shall see that if we are ever saved, it will not be through our own goodness, but through God's infinite grace."[3]

Jesus. Only. All.

Everything depends on Jesus—our justification in the past, when we accepted what He did for us on the cross; our sanctification in the present as we grow into His likeness; and our glorification in the future, when we will be escorted to our eternal home. It is not "our work plus God's work" that saves, transforms, and glorifies us. NO, NO, NO! It is God's work. All of it. Period. Apart from accepting the gift of Jesus, we can do nothing to be saved or remain saved.

Salvation is the work of Jesus—past, present, and future.

As you contemplate your eternal destiny and where you are ultimately going, you may despair that you're not good enough to get there. And in that assessment you would be right: You are not good enough. But Jesus is. Accept Him, and you will be saved. Your salvation leaves no room for doubt. The Bible is so clear:

"God has given us eternal life, and this life is in his Son. Whoever has the Son has life; whoever does not have the Son of God does not have life" (1 John 5:11, 12).

But doubts can creep in. Perhaps it is because we do not trust Jesus to transform us. To save us? Sure, that is an act of grace, a gift that we cannot earn. But to change us? To become better people? We've got to at least try, right?

Wrong. The problem with the "trying" plan is that every time you screw up, you doubt your salvation. That is because it's hard to accept that character change comes solely by trusting in Jesus. It is a gift. Jesus changes us. All we can do is trust Him. For those of us raised on the maxim, "Don't just sit there, do something," this is counter-intuitive. For grace teaches, in a way, "Don't just do something, sit there."

Recently I posted some of these ideas on my Facebook page. I must have hit a soft spot, because more than 100 friends replied. Here is that blog:

"In my quiet time today I read this statement from W. W. Prescott (*Victory in Christ*, p. 25): 'For a long time I tried to obtain victory over sin, and I failed. I have since discovered the reason. Instead of doing the part which God expects me to do and which I can do and which He cannot do for me, I was trying to do God's part which He does not expect me to do and which I cannot do and which He has promised to do for me.'

"My reflection: 'If anyone is in Christ he is a new creature.' I have been trying harder to be a new creature than I have been trying to be in Christ. Don't fight sin. Find Christ."

Once Saved, Always Saved, So Long as You Stay Saved in Jesus

So what is the one thing you—and only you—can do to find victory over sin? The answer is simple: Surrender to Jesus. That, then, empowers Jesus to do the one thing we cannot do for ourselves: Transform the heart.

Keep this in mind next time you're tempted to question your salvation: God does not want you to be fuzzy about being saved. Paul explains:

"Just one trespass resulted in condemnation for all people, so also one righteous act resulted in justification and life for all people" (Rom. 5:18).

In other words, because of what Jesus did on the cross, if you accept Him as your Savior, you are saved. Period.

God loves you no matter what you do. You will never behave good enough to earn His love, and you will never sin bad enough to erase His love. In the words of Jerry Bridges:

"Your worst days are never so bad that you are beyond the reach of God's grace. And your best days are never so good that you are beyond the need of God's grace."

So does it follow that we should "go on sinning so that grace may increase" (Rom. 6:1)? Paul answers, "By no means" (verse. 2)! Other translations put it this way: "God forbid" (KJV), "Of course not!" (TLB), "No! No!" (NEB), "Oh what a ghastly thought!" (Phillips).

The point is that in Christ we are sanctified. We gain freedom from sin. It is not to suggest that we never mess up, as the Bible makes it clear that we all sin. But such sin is not about doing bad things—it is always about disconnecting from Jesus. When we cease to abide in Christ, we sin. But when we stay in Christ, we are always saved—even when we engage in bad behaviors.

The metaphor I like on this point is to think of riding up in an elevator. In Christ you are going upward, to heaven. At times you may fall, but so long as you're in the elevator, you're still headed the right direction. Remember that the next time you stumble spiritually. As long as you are in Christ, you're still heading to heaven.

One author uses the illustration of driving over a bridge. Let's say you head across the Golden Gate Bridge with perfect faith that it will hold you, and you arrive safely on the other side.

With faith just as strong, now let's say you drive onto some wooden bridge that then collapses because the boards are decayed. As a result, you crash into the creek. Thus it is not your sincerity, or even your faith, that keeps you safe. It is the object of your faith that made the difference. If you place all the faith in the world in a religious system, in your willpower, or in your churchy behaviors, you will be lost. But the smallest amount of faith in the Lord Jesus Christ assures your salvation.

How, then, do works fit into this scenario? Let's return to the Golden Gate Bridge. When initially constructed, it had no safety net in place. During the first phase of the construction 23 men fell to their death. Finally a bright engineer suggested that they put a net beneath the bridge. For the modest price of $100,000 they installed the net.

During the second half of the construction 10 men fell. All of them were saved in the net. But what's amazing is that production increased 25 percent! Why? Because once people knew that they could work—and even fall—without fear of death, they did better work.

Your heavenly Father does not want you to live with the fear of falling. He is your bridge to heaven, and He wants you to know that there is a net in the shape of a cross anchored beneath you, securing you in your salvation. And in that assurance you can do better work.

Royal Assurance

Queen Victoria once attended a service in St. Paul's Cathedral and listened to a sermon with keen interest. Afterward she asked her chaplain, "Can one be absolutely sure in this life of eternal safety?" He answered that he knew no way that one could be totally sure.

The incident, published in the *Court News,* came to the notice of a minister named John Townsend. After reading of Queen Victoria's question and the answer she received, he prayed and then sent the following note to her:

"To Her Gracious Majesty, our beloved Queen Victoria, from one of her most humble subjects: With trembling hands, but heart-filled love, and because I know that we can be absolutely sure now for our eternal life in the home that Jesus went to prepare, may I ask Your Most Gracious Majesty to read the following passages of Scripture: John 3:16, Romans 10:9-10. . . . I sign myself, your servant for Jesus' sake, John Townsend."

About two weeks later he received the following letter: "To John Townsend: . . . I have carefully and prayerfully read the portions of Scripture referred to. I believe in the finished work of Christ for me, and trust, by God's grace, to meet you in that home of which He said, 'I go to prepare a place for you.' (Signed) Victoria Guelph."

After Queen Victoria's discovery of Christian assurance, she used to carry a small booklet titled *Safety, Certainty, and Enjoyment.* It is what she found in Christ. And so can you.

---

[1] Billy Graham, *Death and the Life After* (Nashville: Thomas Nelson, 1987), pp. 93-95.

[2] Frederick Buechner, as quoted in www.stmarks-cb.org/joomla-1.5/index.php?option=com_content&view=article&id=206:111608--zephaniah-17-18-1-thessalonians-51-10-matthew-2514-29&catid=13:sermons-by-rev-mark-giroux&Itemid=31 (accessed Apr. 1, 2012).

[3] Ellen G. White, *Christ's Object Lessons* (Battle Creek, Mich.: Review and Herald Pub. Assn., 1900), p. 159.

Safe at Home

Harvard professor Steven Pinker marvels at the workings of the brain. In a *Time* magazine article, "The Mystery of Consciousness," he suggests that a brain is all we have—that is, we possess no eternal soul. He writes:

"And when you think about it, the doctrine of a life-to-come is not such an uplifting idea after all because it necessarily devalues life on earth. ... Think, too, about why we sometimes remind ourselves that 'life is short.' It is an impetus to extend a gesture of affection to a loved one, to bury the hatchet in a pointless dispute, to use time productively rather than squander it. I would argue that nothing gives life more purpose than the realization that every moment of consciousness is a precious and fragile gift."[1]

I'm no hotshot Harvard brain, but I would argue against one. Of course we should treasure every moment, but to suggest that the belief in a life to come devalues a life today is akin to arguing that if I believe there's a hot fudge sundae to follow my meal, then the baked potato has no point. To see this life as a small taste of a much better life to come doesn't discredit the deliciousness of today. It simply interprets today through the hopeful lens of a better tomorrow. Such a worldview enlightens our lives and puts death into its proper context. Listen to how Paul expresses his pity for Steven Pinker:

"If only for this life we have hope in Christ, we are of all people most to be pitied" (1 Cor. 15:19).

Scripture teaches that God has "set eternity in the human heart" (Eccl. 3:11). The psalmist adds, "But the plans of the Lord stand firm forever, the purposes of his heart through all generations" (Ps. 33:11). God has a plan and a purpose for you. Not only for today, but also for forever!

Focusing solely on this life is like going to the Super Bowl and leaving right after the performance of "The Star-Spangled Banner." Sure, you enjoyed the warm-ups, and the practice drills were entertaining; the kickers wowed you by how far they could kick field goals (when the ball sat on a tee and there was no pressure). But you skipped the real game. Thus you missed the whole purpose for which you were there. The present life is warm-up for the one to come. It's the sample on a pink spoon at Baskin-Robbins, not the ice-cream cone itself.

Paul reminds us that God made us for the purpose of eternity. Drawing on the metaphors of buildings and clothing, he explains that our time on this earth is a temporary deal:

"For we know that if the earthly tent we live in is destroyed, we have a building from God, an eternal house in heaven, not built by human hands. Meanwhile we groan, longing to be clothed instead with our heavenly dwelling, because when we are clothed, we will not be found naked. For while we are in this tent, we groan and are burdened, because we do not wish to be unclothed but to be clothed instead with our heavenly dwelling, so that what is mortal may be swallowed up by life. Now the one who has fashioned us for this very purpose is God, who has given us the Spirit as a deposit, guaranteeing what is to come" (2 Cor. 5:1-5).

You are God's treasure, fashioned for one purpose: to be with Him for eternity.

Recently I read the story of Violet Bailey and her fiancé, Samuel Booth. Back in 1941 they were strolling through the English countryside, deeply in love and engaged to be married. A diamond engagement ring sparkled on Violet's finger—her most treasured possession.

Then one of them made a hurtful barb. An argument ensued, then escalated. Violet became so angry that she chucked her diamond engagement ring into the field. The ring lodged in the grass in such a way that it was impossible to see. Violet and Samuel kissed and made up. Then they searched and searched for the ring, but to no avail.

Two months later they got married. They had a child and then a grandson. Part of their family lore was the story of that lost engagement ring.

Violet and Samuel celebrated their fiftieth wedding anniversary. In 1993 Samuel died. Another 15 years passed, but the ring was not forgotten. One day Violet's grandson got an idea: Perhaps he could find his grandmother's ring with a metal detector. After crisscrossing the field for two hours, he discovered the treasure that had been buried for 67 years.

Nothing in his life compared to that moment when he slid the diamond ring on his astonished grandma's finger. Violet was overwhelmed beyond words. The treasured possession had come home.

You and I are God's treasured possession. Sin has separated us from Him. We are not where we are supposed to be—not on this earth, not in this state of sin. So we groan. Sure, we encounter glorious glimpses of God during this pilgrimage. We experience fragments of eternity on this earth. The journey does have its moments of immense joy. But compared to what lies ahead, when we will be reunited with our Father, this is just time in the dirt. Someday we will be home.[2]

Recently I saw a breathtaking video of the constellation Orion, set to "I Will Bring you Home," by Michael Card. Tears drenched my eyes as I thought of our journey someday through Orion to that place where we will be with our Father forever. We will be home.

While watching that video, I remembered a phone call my dad had received when I was a boy.

It came at 3:00 in the morning. Still half asleep, my dad managed a confused "Hello?"

"Isn't it wonderful, Pastor?" the aged voice said excitedly.

"Huh? What are you talking about?" My dad figured he had to be dreaming.

"Have you looked outside, Pastor?"

"What are you talking about?" My dad peered outside into the darkness.

"Just look," the elderly woman persisted. "It's dark! It's dark, Pastor. This is it!"

"Yeah? So?"

"No more arthritis! No more glaucoma! No more wheelchair! Soon I'll be in my new heavenly body. Jesus is here at last!"

"Mrs. Charles," my dad said gently, beginning to understand. "Do you know it's 3:00 in the *morning?*"

"Huh? No, Pastor, it's 3:00 in the afternoon, and look how dark it is! Jesus is coming. All things are made new."

"No, Mrs. Charles. It's nighttime. That's why it's dark outside."

"Are you sure, Pastor?"

"Yes, Mrs. Charles."

"Oh, Pastor, I'm terribly sorry. I thought it was the afternoon and . . . I mean, I just assumed Jesus was . . . what I'm saying is . . . I feel so silly. I'm sorry. It must be this new medication Dr. Darcy put me on. Oh, Pastor, you go back to bed. I'm sorry. Good night."

I wish I could say Jesus came that night and took Mrs. Charles home. I wish that that evening God had destroyed her wheelchair and smoothed her wrinkles and restored the bounce in her step as she sailed toward heaven.

But Mrs. Charles is dead now. Her home has been replaced with an Exxon mini mart.

A few years ago, when I visited the old New England church where I had known Mrs. Charles, many pews were empty. The years have eroded the storybook church of my memories. I wish I could report of a vibrant church . . . but I can't.

I wish I could make that church new again. I wish I could return to kindergarten and sing "Happy, Happy Home," and grimace at the slobbery greetings of the old women, and fidget in the pew during my dad's sermon. I wish I could restore the vigor and enthusiasm as I remember it . . . but I can't.

I wish I could rebuild the neighborhood I grew up in. I'd replace the gangs with the carefree kids I remember. I'd exchange the drug dealers that now rule Johnston Creek Park with the Little Leaguers of my childhood. If I could make all things new, I would ... but I can't.

But God can.

So I will tenaciously hold to His promise: "Now we look forward with confidence to our heavenly bodies, realizing that every moment we spend in these earthly bodies is time spent away from our eternal home in heaven with Jesus" (2 Cor. 5:6, TLB).

Of course, even in our earthly bodies we taste appetizers that make us hungry for heaven. Connections with BFFs, encounters with people at the soup kitchen, romantic getaways, aromas of the Thanksgiving feast, snow days, concerts in Carnegie Hall, reconciliations with rivals, belly laughs, praying with children—there are numerous delectable samples of the life to come. They are restrained and too infrequent on this earth, but they exist just the same. Even in this shady, sin-saturated, Son-starved world we find moments when a beam of light from heaven illuminates our darkness.

Appetizers like that make me hungry for heaven. Connections with my dad, encounters with people at the soup kitchen, romantic getaways, aromas of the Thanksgiving feast, snow days, concerts in Carnegie Hall, reconciliations with rivals, belly laughs, praying with the kids—there are numerous delectable samples of the life to come. They are restrained and too infrequent on this earth, but they exist just the same. Even in this shady, sin-saturated, Son-starved world we find moments when a beam of light from heaven illuminates our darkness.

In his talk "The Sense of an Ending" Jeremy Begbie, a professor from Duke University, shared his experience of attending a worship service in a poor South African township. He was aware that the worshippers gathered had recently suffered horrendous pain and loss. That week a tornado had destroyed 50 homes in the township. Five people had died. The day before, a local gang had stabbed and killed a Sunday school member—a 14-year-old. Clearly you'd have had a hard time finding any heaven in church on that morning.

The pastor began with prayer: "Lord, You are Creator and Sovereign, but why did the wind come like a snake and tear our roofs off? Why did a mob cut short the life of one of our own children, when he had everything to live for? Over and over again, Lord, we are in the midst of death."

As he prayed, the congregation groaned laboriously. When he finished, the people began to sing. At first their music subdued, mournful. But their songs mounted toward a crescendo of praise to the God, who has plunged into the very worst of humanity in order to give us a reason to sing. They sang of a brighter ending to our story of suffering.

"The singing gave that congregation a foretaste of the end," Begbie said. He went on to explain: "Christian hope isn't about looking around at the state of things now and trying to imagine where it's all going. It's not about trying to calculate the future from the present. It's about breathing now the fresh air of the ending, tasting the spices . . . of the feast to come."[3]

Yes, both evil and beauty fills our world. The evil blasts brutal reminders that we are not home yet. Still, the beauty comes in refreshing breaths that give our lives an air of a better life to come.

And so we press on. But as followers of Christ, we do not walk blindly. We know where we are going and can smell it, taste it, feel it, see it. In reality, we are going home.

---

[1] Steven Pinker, "The Mystery of Consciousness," *Time*, Jan. 29, 2007, p. 70.

[2] "It Wasn't All Bad," *The Week*, Feb. 15, 2008.

[3] Dallas Willard, ed., *A Place for Truth* (Downer's Grove, Ill.: InterVarsity Press, 2010), p. 232.

A Trip That's
Out of This World

What is your destiny? Asked another way, "What is your destination?" Anyone who has traveled knows how important it is to get to the right destination. Just last week I was on a flight from Dayton to Denver. Before closing the cabin door the flight attendant announced, "This is United Airlines Flight 3711 to Denver. If Denver is not in your travel plans, please step forward, and we will help you get to your intended destination." Either we appeared to be particularly clueless or the flight attendant wanted quadruple insurance that we understood the import of her words, because she repeated that announcement four times!

A destination—that is, a destiny—is a most important consideration. As Yogi Berra once quipped: "You've got to be very careful if you don't know where you're going, because you might not get there."

Where are you going? What is your destination?

I happened on a blog that put it this way:

"'Life is all about the journey, not the destination!' I saw this sign at the airport today. Imagine, in an airport of all places!

"What stupidity! Tell passengers arriving at the airport to catch a flight, 'Take any flight, sir, it doesn't matter; it's not about your destination, it's only about the experience of the flight.'

"I don't know about you, but if it's only about the journey, then life is ultimately a sadistic, cruel, cosmic joke, and I want off!

"But I know better. Life is a journey in preparation to arrive at the destination, which is all-important. My destination is heaven and union with God for eternity."[1]

The Bible teaches this truth. Anticipating our final destination, John the revelator writes:

"And I heard a loud voice from the throne saying, 'Look! God's dwelling place is now among the people, and he will dwell with them. They will be his people, and God himself will be with them and be their God'" (Rev. 21:3).

Heaven. That is our destination.

Seems everybody is talking about heaven these days. Want a best seller? Put "heaven" in the title. *The Five People You Meet in Heaven*, by Mitch Albom; *Heaven*, by Randy Alcorn; *90 Minutes in Heaven*, by Cecil B. Murphey and Don Piper; *Heaven Is for Real*, by Phil Rehberg; *The Boy Who Came Back From Heaven*, by Kevin Malarkey; *Letters to Heaven*, by Calvin Miller; and *Glimpses of Heaven*, by Trudy Harris—all are blockbusters at the bookstore that aim to scratch our heavenly itch. Makes me wonder if I should reconsider the title of this book (*HEAVEN and Destiny: Who You Are and What You're Here to Do and a Really Important Chapter About HEAVEN and Although I've Never Been to HEAVEN, HEAVEN Is a Place Called HEAVEN, Where I Hope to Go*—or something like that).

I just finished reading the current best seller, *Heaven Is for Real: A Little Boy's Astounding Story of His Trip to Heaven and Back.* (Maybe that's my title: *Heaven Is for Real: A Big Boy's Astounding Story of His Reading "Heaven Is for Real: A Little Boy's Astounding Story of His Trip to Heaven and Back".* . .) It's the story of 3-year-old Colton Burpo, the son of a Wesleyan pastor in Imperial, Nebraska, who was rushed into emergency surgery with a burst appendix. Colton awoke with an incredible story: He said that he had died and gone to heaven, where he met his great-grandfather, the biblical figure Samson, John the Baptist, and Jesus, who had eyes that "were just sort of a sea-blue and they seemed to sparkle."

It sounds implausible, doesn't it? Although my dragon of doubt was inflamed as I read the book, I must admit that there was a deep yearning within me, aching for the story to be true. While my default mode is to cater to cynicism, I couldn't squelch my ravenous hunger for heaven. I want to possess a childlike faith in a better world beyond this one.

C. S. Lewis offers a helpful explanation for my befuddled feelings:

"The Christian says, 'Creatures are not born with desires unless satisfaction for those desires exists.' A baby feels hunger: well, there is such a thing as food. Men feel sexual desire: well, there is such a thing as sex. If I find in myself a desire which no experience in this world can satisfy, the most probable explanation is that I was made for another world."[2]

No question that I desire a destination beyond the present world. Why? Well, I wasn't designed to live here. I was made for another world.

Imagine someone giving you an Indy race car. You jump in that baby faster than the speed of light. Helmeting up and buckling down, you race to the closest interstate . . . only to find bumper-to-bumper congestion. That's when the awful truth hits you: Your $7 million mobile isn't much good in a traffic jam. Impatiently you massage the $50,000 steering wheel and suck the exhaust of the Kia Rio that sits in front of you. And you keep restarting your engine. Come to find out, the car can't just sit and idle—it sputters and coughs. Why? Because the car was not designed to sit and sound pretty. It was created to accelerate from 0 to 100 mph in three seconds and curve a corner at 200 mph. Until you let that car perform in a way that is consistent with its design, you're only going to be frustrated.

Similarly, you and I were not fashioned for this earth. Yes, sometimes this feels frustrating. Paul laments this reality as he ponders the hereafter. He writes:

"For now we see only a reflection as in a mirror; then we shall see face to face. Now I know in part; then I shall know fully, even as I am fully known" (1 Cor. 13:12).

Only when we are with God, in heaven, will we reach our destiny—that is, our destination.

Friend, the day is coming when you will fully flourish in the environment for which God created you. You were made for another world.

"Our world isn't a very good amusement park," observes Paul David Tripp. "No, it's a broken place groaning for redemption. Here is meant to make us long for forever. Here is meant to prepare us for eternity."[3]

Don't settle into this world too comfortably, for it is not your final destination. As good as it is, it's chalk dust compared to what's coming.

Snail Talk

An old legend tells of a swan and a crane. A beautiful swan swooped by the banks of a pond where a crane was wading about, seeking snails. For a few moments the crane viewed the swan in stupid wonder and then asked, "Where do you come from?"

"I come from heaven!" replied the swan.

"And where is heaven?"

"Heaven!" the swan exclaimed, "Heaven! Have you never heard of heaven?" The beautiful bird described the grandeur of the eternal city. She told of streets of gold and gates and walls made of precious stones. Dreamily she described the river of life flowing as pure as crystal. In eloquent terms the swan depicted the tree of life and the hosts who live in the other world—yet failed to arouse the slightest interest on the part of the crane.

Finally the crane asked: "Are there any snails there?"

"Snails!" gasped the swan, "No! Of course there are not."

"Then," said the crane, as it continued its search along the slimy banks of the pond, "you can have your heaven. I want snails!"

I wonder how often we get distracted by the trinkets and toys of this world—even though they're slimy snails compared to what is yet to come. Listen up, and you'll hear high-powered prattle that seems to be important, but in reality it's snail talk.

"Check out my new set of wheels!"

"My new iPad rocks."

"We're going to Cancun for spring break."

"I can open my garage door with my cell phone. It's the coolest thing ever!"

Let's face it—the stuff that so enamors us is meaningless compared to what is coming. The Bible declares:

"No eye has seen, . . . no ear has heard, and . . . no human mind has conceived the things God has prepared for those who love him" (1 Cor. 2:9).

Ellen White offers this commentary: "Paul had a view of heaven, and in discoursing on the glories there, the very best thing he could do was to not try to describe them. He tells us that eye had not seen nor ear heard, neither hath it entered into the heart of man the things which God hath prepared for those that love Him. So you may put your imagination to the stretch, you may try to the very best of your abilities to take in and consider the eternal weight of glory, and yet your finite senses, faint and weary with the effort, cannot grasp it, for there is an infinity beyond."[4]

Moving Beyond the Snail Tale

Calvin Miller tells of a man who loved "the sunny country of common sense," but he could not grasp "the mysteries of godliness." Miller kept trying to show him that the mysteries held the meaning of faith. One day the man said, "Pastor, you know this new eternal life I have—well, I've been thinking about it. What are we going to do all day long for eternity? Play harps on clouds?"

"No," said Miller. "We'll praise the Lord. Forever—for 10 million years!"

The man was not impressed. "We're going to stand around and praise the Lord?"

"Well, yes," Miller replied, thinking his pitch on heaven was starting to sound like an infomercial.

The man persisted. "Praising God for millions and millions of years? That's it?"

"Um, well, yeah."

"You think maybe we could stop now and then and just mess around awhile?"

Although Miller kidded him about his "dumb questions," later he reflected on his own similar questions. Eventually he reached this conclusion: How meager our understanding of heaven!

Indeed the human mind struggles to fathom the hereafter. But make no mistake—heaven is in our blood. It is our birthright, our destination. To dismiss your ultimate destiny because you do not have the words to describe it or the insight to comprehend it is to commit the unpardonable sin of purpose.

You must understand your purpose on this earth within the broader construct of our final destination. When seen in that framework, your story is so much bigger than the short chapter on this earth. As C. S. Lewis said: "If you read history you will find that the Christians who did most for the present world were just those who thought most of the next. . . . Aim at heaven and you will get earth 'thrown in': aim at earth and you will get neither."

This trip is taking you to heaven. If heaven is not in your travel plans, please step forward and get help so you can arrive at your intended destination.

Please read that last paragraph four times.

---

[1] www.catholic-convert.com/2012/02/24/life-is-about-the-journey-not-the-destination-huh/ (accessed Mar. 12, 2012).

[2] http://blogs.mymedifast.com/Blogs/ejmenard/Archive/2011/10/12/858837.aspx (accessed Mar. 12, 2012).

[3] Paul David Tripp, *Forever: Why You Can't Live Without It* (Grand Rapids: Zondervan, 2011), p. 39.

[4] Ellen G. White, *Sermons and Talks* (Silver Spring, Md.: E. G. White Estate, 1990), vol. 1, p. 73.

Con**clusion**

"The bottom line is in heaven!"

—Edwin H. Land

"Here now is my final conclusion: Fear God and obey his commands, for this is everyone's duty."

—Ecclesiastes 12:13, NLT

*"The way you get meaning into your life
is to devote yourself to loving others,
devote yourself to your community around you,
and devote yourself to creating something
that gives you purpose and meaning."*

—Mitch Albom

*"Life without a purpose is a languid, drifting thing;
every day we ought to review our purpose, saying to ourselves, 'This day
let me make a sound beginning,
for what we have hitherto done is naught!'"*

—Thomas à Kempis

*"Remember, dear young friends, that each day, each hour, each moment,
you are weaving the web of your own destiny."*

—Ellen G. White

Po or Purpose?

In the movie *Kung Fu Panda,* a panda named Po wants desperately to learn kung fu. But many obstacles loom between him and his dream—not the least of which is the father who wants Po to take over the family's restaurant business.

"Sorry, Dad," Po says as he descends the stairs from his room to the kitchen of the family restaurant.

"Sorry doesn't make the noodles," his father replies. "What were you doing up there? All that noise?"

"Oh, nothing," Po answers. "Just had a crazy dream."

Suddenly his dad's interest is piqued. "What were you dreaming about?" he wonders.

"What was I—? Uhhhh . . . " Po struggles to find an answer because he was dreaming about kung fu. He knows his father would disapprove of it, so he lies:

"I was dreaming about . . . uh . . . noodles."

"Noodles?" his father remarked, thrilled. "You were really dreaming about noodles? . . . Oh, happy day!" he exclaims. "My son is finally having the Noodle Dream! You don't know how long I have been waiting for this moment!" He places an official restaurant cap on Po's head.

"This is a sign, Po!" his father exclaims.

"Uh . . . a sign of what?" a confused Po asks.

"You are almost ready to be entrusted with the secret ingredient to my Secret Ingredient Soup! And then you will fulfill your destiny and take over the restaurant—just as I took it over from my father, who took it over from his father, who won it from a friend in a game of mahjong."

"Dad, Dad, Dad," Po says, trying to stem his father's enthusiasm. "It was just a dream."

"No, it was *the* dream. We are noodle folk, Po. Broth runs through our veins!"

"But, Dad, didn't you ever want to do something else? Something besides noodles?"

"Actually," his father admits, "when I was young and crazy, I thought about running away and learning how to make tofu."

"So why didn't you?"

"Because it was a stupid dream. Can you imagine me making tofu? Ha! No, we all have our place in this world. Mine is here, and yours is—."

"I know," Po interrupts. "Mine is here."

"No, it's at tables 2, 5, 7, and 12. Service with a smile!"[1]

Got Any Po in Ya?

Has God planted a dream in your heart that others are quick to write off as "stupid" or "silly"? Are you tempted to settle for a lesser dream in order to squelch the skeptics' voices? Do you allow the opinions of others to dwarf the God-sized dreams that keep you awake at night?

One thing you can count on: Satan does not want you to fulfill God's destiny for your life, and he will unleash hell's fury to destroy your dream.

Some time ago I lived in South Africa for a year. My weekends followed a typical routine: Finish work around noon on Friday, then beeline it to Kruger National Park and drive around until Sunday night, photographing wild animals. I still remember something a park ranger told me on one of those outings. He explained how lions would stalk pregnant wildebeests, patiently waiting in the shadows until the birth day. Just as mama wildebeest would go into labor, the lion would pounce. The defenseless mother and calf made for easy prey.

That image has come to mind through the years whenever I felt ready to give birth to a dream. Inevitably, the evil one's most vicious attacks seemed carefully timed to coincide with a personal, spiritual breakthrough.

Scripture warns that "the devil prowls around like a roaring lion looking for someone to devour. Resist him" (1 Peter 5:8, 9).

As you dream about God's calling in your life, don't give in. How? The answer is right there in the passage. Just before the command is this verse: "Cast all your anxiety on him because he cares for you" (verse 7). Then the verses that follow say, "Resist him, standing firm in the faith. . . . And the God of all grace, who called you to his eternal glory in Christ, after you have suffered a little while, will himself restore you and make you strong, firm and steadfast" (verses 9, 10). Note that you do not need spiritual muscle to survive the devil's attacks. No! What you need is Jesus.

The only way to stay on course with your calling is to remain connected to Jesus. Put your fears on Him. Place your faith in Him. Let He who "has called you to his eternal glory" transform you. The text says that it's God's job to make you "strong, firm and steadfast"—not yours. Trust Him to do what He says He will do. Your only job is to stay connected to Him through prayer, time in the Word, and service to others. Do those three things, and you'll be on the right track.

What Voice?

Focus on your relationship with Jesus. Don't listen to the vicious voices that would disparage your dream. Isn't it time to stop obsessing about the opinions of others and tune in to the guidance of God instead? Jessie Rice, in *The Church of Facebook*, published his intention to "break up with" his fear of what others think about him. He writes:

"Dear Fear-of-What-Others-Think,

"I am sick of you, and it's time we broke up. I know we've broken up and gotten back together about a bazillion times, but seriously, Fear-of-What-Others-Think (or FOWOT, for short), *this is it*. We're breaking up.

"Because I'm tired of overthinking my status updates on Facebook, trying to sound more clever, funny, important. And I'm tired of wondering which Tweets might drive the most traffic to my blog, as though my value as a human being were truly numerical. . . .

"I'm sick of feeling anxious about what I say or do in public, especially around people I don't know that well, all in the hope that they'll like me, accept me, praise me . . . Like me! Like me! Like me! . . .

"And all of this is especially horrible, terrible, evil because if I really stop and think about it, and let things go quiet and listen patiently for the voice of the God who made me and delights in me, it turns out I'm actually—*profoundly*—precious, lovable, worthy, valuable, and even just a little ghetto-fabulous.

"When I listen to *that* voice then *your* voice starts to sound ridiculous again. You turn back into the tiny, whining little wiener dog that you are.

"So . . . you and I are done. And no, I'm not interested in 'talking it through.' I'm running, jumping, laughing you out of my life, once and for all. Or at least that's what I really, really want, God help me."[2]

Need to File for Divorce?

Got anything you need to say to FOWOT? I hope our journey together has given you the confidence to divorce those nagging doubts that diminish your self-worth and measure your value by superficial symbols. Your significance goes far beyond the number of followers you have on Twitter, the size of your portfolio or the square footage in your corner office. Rather, you are a child of God—a saint with a destiny that stretches far beyond this world. It means that your pilgrimage through the present world is packed with purpose. You are here for a reason, called to glorify God in all things. Your contribution to the greater good of humankind may be but two mites, but your donation to the world is significant nonetheless and should not be undervalued. So look beyond yourself and see the grander purpose for which God created you. Use this life to prepare for the next.

Consider King David's epitaph: "David . . . served God's purpose in his own generation" (Acts 13:36). The "man after God's own heart" made the most of his life. He fulfilled the divine intent in his generation.

Now it's your turn, your generation, and your opportunity to fulfill God's purpose in a contemporary and timely way.

Can You Answer the Big Questions?

As you live in Christ, you can fulfill God's purpose in your life. In so doing, you will discover the answers to the big questions we have considered. You will know who you are, why you are here, and where you are going.

In January 2000, leaders of Charlotte, North Carolina, invited their favorite son, Billy Graham, to a luncheon. Graham hesitated to accept the invitation because of his struggles with Parkinson's disease, but the Charlotte leaders said, "We don't expect a major address. Just come and let us honor you." So he agreed.

After people had said wonderful things, Graham stepped to the rostrum, looked at the crowd, and said, "I'm reminded today of Albert Einstein, the great physicist who this month has been honored by *Time* magazine as the Man of the Century. Einstein was once traveling from Princeton on a train when the conductor came down the aisle, punching the tickets of each passenger. When he came to Einstein, Einstein reached in his vest pocket. He couldn't find his ticket, so he reached in his other pocket. It wasn't there, so he looked in his briefcase but couldn't find it. Then he looked in the seat by him. He couldn't find it. The conductor said,

'Dr. Einstein, I know who you are. We all know who you are. I'm sure you bought a ticket. Don't worry about it.' Einstein nodded appreciatively.

"The conductor continued down the aisle punching tickets. As he was ready to move to the next car, he turned around and saw the great physicist down on his hands and knees looking under his seat for his ticket. The conductor rushed back and said, 'Dr. Einstein, Dr. Einstein, don't worry. I know who you are. No problem. You don't need a ticket. I'm sure you bought one.' Einstein looked at him and said, 'Young man, I too know who I am. What I don't know is where I'm going.'"

Billy Graham continued, "See the suit I'm wearing? It's a brand-new suit. My wife, my children, and my grandchildren are telling me I've gotten a little slovenly in my old age. I used to be a bit more fastidious. So I went out and bought a new suit for this luncheon and one more occasion. You know what that occasion is? This is the suit in which I'll be buried. But when you hear I'm dead, I don't want you to immediately remember the suit I'm wearing. I want you to remember this: I not only know who I am, I also know where I'm going."[3]

Jesus said, "I know where I came from and where I am going" (John 8:14). Stay connected to Jesus, and you can declare with the same confidence:

"I know who I am—a child of God."

"I know why I'm here—to glorify God."

"I know where I'm going—to be with God forever."

---

[1] *Kung Fu Panda* (DreamWorks Animation, 2008), directed by Mark Osborne and John Stevenson, DVD, scene 2, 00:02:29-00:05:18.

[2] Jessie Rice, "'Dear Fear-of-What-Others-Think…': An Open Letter to My Imaginary Audience," http://churchoffacebook.com/ (accessed Mar. 29, 2012).

[3] John Huffman, "Who Are You, and Where Are You Going?" Preaching Conference 2002, www.preachingtoday.com/illustrations/2002/october/13942.html (accessed Apr. 2, 2012).